Reflections of Rebellion

BENSON J. LOSSING

INTRODUCTION BY MICHAEL C. SCOGGINS

Reflections of Rebellion

Hours with the Living Men and Women of *The Revolution*

Published by The History Press
www.historypress.net

Original material used in the production of this book from the collection of Michael C. Scoggins.

First published 1889
The History Press edition 2005
Second printing 2007

Manufactured in the United States

ISBN 978-1-59629-030-3

Library of Congress Cataloging-in-Publication Data

Lossing, Benson John, 1813-1891.
[Hours with the living men and women of the Revolution]
Reflections of rebellion : hours with the living men and women of the Revolution / Benson J. Lossing ; with a new introduction by Michael C. Scoggins.
p. cm.
Originally published as: Hours with the living men and women of the Revolution. 1889.
ISBN 1-59629-030-7 (alk. paper)
1. United States--History--Revolution, 1775-1783--Biography. 2. United States--History--Revolution, 1775-1783--Personal narratives. 3. United States--History--Revolution, 1775-1783--Anecdotes. I. Title.
E206.L67 2005
973.3'092'2--dc22

2005007560

From the Publisher:
This new edition contains the full text from the 1889 text of *Hours with the Living Men and Women of the Revolution*, published by Funk & Wagnalls Publishers. All efforts have been made to maintain the integrity of the original work, including Lossing's spelling, dialect and punctuation.

Contents

Introduction to Benson J. Lossing's *Hours with the Living Men and Women of the Revolution*

Benson John Lossing was born on February 12, 1813, in Beekman, Dutchess County, New York. His parents, John Lossing and Miriam Dorland, were farmers who both died while Lossing was a child. At the age of eleven, with only three years of schooling, Lossing went to work on a neighboring farm, and at age fourteen he became the apprentice of Adam Henderson, a watchmaker and silversmith in Poughkeepsie. The young Lossing had a flair for detailed work and a great deal of natural artistic ability, and after completing his apprenticeship in 1833 he accepted a partnership in the firm and married Henderson's niece, Alice Barritt. Alice died childless in 1855, and the following year Lossing married Helen Sweet, a union that produced four children.

In 1835 Lossing relinquished his partnership and embarked on a career in journalistic publishing. The Poughkeepsie *Telegraph*, a weekly newspaper with a circulation of 2,500, hired him as editor and joint publisher. In an effort to supplement his meager schooling, Lossing began a diligent program of self-education that involved reading extensively, especially in the fields of American history and classical literature. The following year he founded a semimonthly journal called the Poughkeepsie *Casket*, devoted to "polite literature and the arts." He also continued to develop his technical skills by studying wood engraving under J.A. Adams of New York City. Engraving was the chief method for illustrating nineteenth-century publications, and Lossing's artistic abilities contributed to his talent as a natural engraver. In 1838 Lossing accepted the dual position of editor and illustrator of *Family Magazine*, which Nelson Rockefeller later described as "one of the first fully illustrated periodicals published in North America." Lossing also entered into a partnership with his brother-in-law, William Barritt, and the two men founded a wood engraving business in New York City. Lossing and Barritt produced high-quality engravings for both books and periodicals, and within a short time became the leading wood engravers in the state of New York.

In addition to his engraving skills, Lossing also developed a keen interest in history, both local and national, and a strong desire not only to illustrate books but to write them as well. In 1840 his first book, *Outline History of the Fine Arts*, was released as Number 105 of the "Harper's Family Library" series. "It was kindly noticed by the critics," Lossing later recalled, "and, encouraged, I felt a strong desire to make a more pretentious effort in the wide and attractive field of historical literature." A year later, Lossing gave up his publishing responsibilities in Poughkeepsie so that he could concentrate on his own projects. One of Lossing's most passionate interests was military history, especially the American Revolution, and for the rest of his life much of his work would revolve around that theme. His next endeavor was a two-volume study on the beginnings of the Revolution entitled *Seventeen Hundred and Seventy-Six, or The War of Independence*, published in 1846 and 1847, followed by an ambitious biographical anthology, *Lives of the Presidents of the United States*, also published in 1847.

A chance encounter in rural Connecticut in the summer of 1848 would set Lossing on an eight-month-long, nine-thousand-mile trek across the thirteen original United States and parts of Canada, during which he would visit the most famous scenes of the Revolutionary War and conduct firsthand interviews with the few remaining men and women who lived through those tumultuous times. In June of that year, while traveling between Greenwich and Stanford, Connecticut, Lossing met an elderly veteran of the American War of Independence who turned out to be General Ebenezer Mead. During the Revolution, Mead served in both the Connecticut militia and the Continental army, and Lossing spent an enjoyable afternoon listening to the old man reminisce about his experiences in the war. As Lossing later related, the incident made a "deep impression" on him, and he returned to New York with a burning conviction to visit the "animate and inanimate relics of the old war for independence," which he would record in both words and drawings before they vanished forever.

I knew that the invisible fingers of decay, the plow of agriculture, and the behests of Mammon, unrestrained in their operations by the prevailing spirit of our people, would soon sweep away every tangible vestige of the Revolution...I knew that, like stars at dawn which had beamed brightly through a long night, the men of old were fast fading away, and that relics associated with their trials and triumphs would soon be covered up forever.

Lossing pitched the idea to Harper & Brothers, who quickly agreed to publish the work, and this became the genesis for the *Pictorial Field-Book of the American Revolution, or, Illustrations, by Pen and Pencil, of the History, Biography, Scenery, Relics, and Traditions of the War for Independence,* Lossing's most famous work, published in two volumes in 1850 and 1852.

Even by today's standards, the *Pictorial Field-Book of the American Revolution* is an unparalleled work of scholarship and artistry, and it set the tone for much of Lossing's subsequent work. Carefully researched, meticulously documented, copiously indexed and lavishly illustrated with woodcuts made from Lossing's excellent drawings, the *Field-Book* has stood the test of time and continues to be an invaluable resource for scholars of American history in general and the American Revolution in particular. The modern reader must stand in amazement at the determination and fortitude that led Benson Lossing to travel alone from one end of the Atlantic seaboard to the other, never sure where he would find his next meal or lodging for the night. Even more amazing is the fact that Lossing suffered no accidents or illnesses during his sojourn. "God, in his providence, dealt kindly with me, in all that long and devious travel," he later recalled in the introduction to the *Field-Book*, "for I did not suffer sickness for an hour, and no accident befell me on the way." While political events conspired to transport the country headlong toward a bloody civil war, Lossing met only kindness and friendship in his travels. "I never experienced an unkind word or cold repulsion of manner," he stated. "On the contrary, politeness always greeted my first salutation, and, when the object of my visit was announced, hospitality and friendly services were freely bestowed."

From July 1848 until February 1849, Lossing traveled the back roads of North America from Canada to the Carolinas, interviewing and sketching the "living men and women of the Revolution" and, just as importantly, producing high-quality drawings of Revolutionary War battle sites, forts and homeplaces as they appeared in the late 1840s. Along the way he not only preserved the words and memories of many Revolutionary heroes and heroines, but also sketched numerous landscapes that have long since ceased to exist or have changed beyond recognition. For instance, in my own state of South Carolina, Lossing sketched the Great Falls of the Catawba River, a once magnificent waterfall that now lies buried under the waters of Fishing Creek Lake. His sketch of Rocky Mount, the site of a British fort and a hotly contested battle in the summer of 1780 that I recently visited, shows a barren hilltop almost completely stripped of trees by a century of military and civilian use. The drawing also shows a house and some of the outbuildings of the Barkeley family, who lived on Rocky Mount at the time and with whom Lossing stayed while visiting the site. Nature has since reclaimed Rocky Mount and it is now so heavily forested that it bears little resemblance to Lossing's sketch. The historic Barkeley home survived intact until the 1990s, when vandals burned it to the ground. Today much of the Rocky Mount area is under "development," and both the fort site and the battlefield may soon be lost forever unless some effort is made to protect them.

By the late 1840s the surviving witnesses to the Revolution were all in their late eighties or early nineties, and they were growing fewer with each passing year—much like our own World War II and Korean War veterans are today. Benson Lossing was the only American historian of his time who actually made a concerted effort to track down and interview these men and women before they were all gone. Even more unusual, his interviews captured not only the stories of the American Patriots, or Whigs, but also the American Loyalists, or Tories, and in addition to Americans he talked to individuals of French Canadian, British Canadian, English and Scottish ancestry. In fact, Lossing gathered much more material than he could incorporate into the *Field-Book*, and in subsequent years he would mine this wealth of information for other publications, in particular a book that he would call *Hours with the Living Men and Women of the Revolution*.

The two-volume *Field-Book* contained over eleven hundred engravings by Lossing and Barritt and more than fifteen hundred pages of text, and established Lossing as the leading author of illustrated histories and biographies of his day. The book was a remarkable accomplishment, both in accuracy of information and in amount of detail, and has been reprinted many times since its first publication. However, in spite of its wealth of pictures and historical information, the *Field-Book* suffers from the same weaknesses and shortcomings that most nineteenth-century (and many twentieth-century) American histories of the Revolution exhibit.

The first of these shortcomings is an overly romanticized view of the past. Most American historians in Lossing's day viewed the Revolution as an epic struggle between noble, self-sacrificing Patriots and bloodthirsty Indians, diabolical Tories and barbaric British soldiers. These Victorian histories of the Revolution generally make little pretense of objectivity or critical analysis, and present a very one-sided version of the war. The other problem intrinsic to the histories of Lossing and his contemporaries is the lack of primary source documentation. The modern American historian has access to an incredible variety of firsthand accounts, unpublished manuscripts, critical analyses, genealogical research and archaeological evidence related to the Revolution, all readily available in a variety of printed and electronic formats. Lossing and his contemporaries, on the other hand, had to rely for the most part on local and family traditions, old newspaper accounts and the few published histories that were available to them at the time. They usually had little opportunity or desire to cross-check their sources or compare accounts from multiple witnesses, nor did they have the means to examine the correspondence of some of the most important military and political figures of the time.

Nonetheless, the *Pictorial Field-Book of the American Revolution* stands as a monument to Lossing's skill as both an artist and a historian, and it was the first of a series of "Pictorial Field Books" that he would publish in the years to come. In 1854 Lossing released the *Illustrated History of the United States for Schools and Families*, intended for grammar school students and family readers. He followed this a year later with *Our Countrymen, or Brief Memoirs of Eminent Americans*, a collection of biographies of "leading statesmen, patriots, orators and others."

In 1857 Lossing undertook a journey from the Adirondack Mountains down the length of the Hudson River to Sandy Hook, a journey of three hundred miles. Traveling by canoe, rowboat, horseback and shank's mare, Lossing recorded his experiences in both words and pictures, producing 463 illustrations documenting the river and the people who lived along it. This journey resulted in *The Hudson, from the Wilderness to the Sea*, a series of articles that first appeared in the London *Art Journal* in 1860 and 1861 and were subsequently printed in book form by H.B. Nims & Co. in 1866.

Lossing's unabashed admiration for George Washington and his accomplishments resulted in the publication of several works on Washington's life in 1859 and 1860. Lossing wrote and illustrated *Mount Vernon and its Associations*, published in 1859, and he illustrated *Recollections and Private Memoirs of Washington*, a collaboration with Washington's foster son George Washington Parke Custis, in 1860. That same year he edited and annotated *The Diary of George Washington from 1789–1791* and published a three-volume *Life of Washington*, in addition to *The Life and Times of Philip Schuyler*, a biography of a well-known Revolutionary War general and congressman from New York.

The War Between the States provided Lossing with the source material for his next multivolume set, the *Pictorial Field Book of the Civil War*, published between 1866 and 1868. A staunch Unionist, Lossing literally followed in the wake of the Union army between 1861 and 1865, documenting the campaigns of the war and sketching the scenes of important battles. Several modern publishers have combined Lossing's text with Matthew Brady's photographs of the war and have reissued this work under various titles such as *Matthew Brady's Illustrated History of the Civil War*. In 1868 Lossing revisited the republic's formative years with the *Pictorial Field Book of the War of 1812*.

In spite of his growing fame with the American public as an author of popular histories and biographies, Lossing was sometimes criticized by the academic establishment for his lack of scholarly credentials and his folksy, conversational style of writing. His status received a boost in 1873 when the University of Michigan awarded him the honorary degree Doctor of Laws (LLD). But privately Lossing resented the arrogance of the academic establishment, and while he could not match their professional credentials, his literary output dwarfed that of his contemporaries and made him the most widely read American historian of his day.

The difficult years of Reconstruction did little to heal the terrible wounds of the Civil War, and as the hundredth anniversary of American independence approached, Lossing began working on a book that would highlight the remarkable achievements of the nation's first century. Entitled *The American Centenary: A History of the Progress of the Republic of the United States during the First One Hundred Years of Its Existence* and published in 1876, the book reflected the pervasive sense of "manifest destiny" that colored most American histories of its time. American history remained the theme for Lossing's next effort, the massive *Cyclopedia of United States History* (1881). He then revisited his home state with the *History of New York City* (1884) and *The Empire State, a Compendious History of the Commonwealth of New York* (1887).

To mark the fortieth anniversary of his original trek to locate the people and places of the American Revolution, Lossing decided to review the copious notes and drawings he had made during his first journey between 1848 and 1849. Many of these stories and sketches had remained unpublished, so Lossing took the opportunity to share some more of them with his readers. He also enlisted the services of another artist, H. Rosa, to recreate in sketches some of the events described by the men and women he had interviewed. Thus was born *Hours with the Living Men and Women of the Revolution: A Pilgrimage*, published by Funk & Wagnalls in New York and London in 1889. Unfortunately, *Hours* was not as successful as many of Lossing's other histories, and only one edition was ever printed. Hence the book is hard to find today, and copies are rare and expensive. It is very exciting, then, that The History Press of Charleston, South Carolina, should reprint it now, in time for the 225th anniversary of many of the events witnessed by the men and women whom Lossing interviewed.

Hours with the Living Men and Women of the Revolution contains some fascinating stories and sketches. Here the reader will find Flora MacDonald, the heroine of the Scottish Highlands who saved Bonnie Prince Charlie from the English hangman in 1745, then fled to North Carolina and faithfully supported the British Crown during the American Revolution. Here are the reminiscences of William McElwees, the last survivor of General Thomas Sumter's Partisan Brigade, who lived within sight of the famous King's Mountain battleground where he and his fellow militiamen defeated the British army under Major Patrick Ferguson. Here is the story of François Vest, who as a young French Canadian lad ran errands for the French General Montcalm as he campaigned against the British General Burgoyne. Here is a sketch of Rebecca Motte, the Revolutionary War heroine from South Carolina who helped General Francis Marion's soldiers set her own house on fire in order to drive out the British troops occupying it. Here are the adventures of Sergeant Uzal Knapp, the last remaining veteran of General George Washington's Life Guards. Lossing's interest even extended to the African Americans and Native Americans so often neglected by Victorian historians of the Revolution. At Arlington House, overlooking the Potomac River and the city of Washington, D.C., he interviewed Eleanor, one of the last of George Washington's many slaves. Although set free after Washington's death, she continued to serve his descendants faithfully even as she approached ninety years of age. In the Wyoming Valley of northeastern Pennsylvania, Lossing spoke with several survivors of the infamous "Wyoming Massacre," a raid on Whig settlements conducted by Tories and Indians in July 1778. Among those he met was Frances Slocum, who was abducted by Delaware Indians, raised as an Indian, married an Indian and was finally reunited with her white family sixty years after her captivity. All together, there are twenty-one stories in *Hours with the Living Men and Women of the Revolution*, each of them fascinating in its own right and a valuable addition to the firsthand accounts of the Revolutionary War.

Even as he approached the last year of his life, Lossing remained as indefatigable and productive as ever. The year 1890 saw him publish his most ambitious work yet, *The Achievements of Four Centuries; or, The Wonderful Story of Our Great Continent within and beyond the States*. Covering the entire scope of American history, Lossing drew on all his years of research and travel and his compendious volumes of notes and drawings to produce what would be his most monumental effort. On June 3, 1891, at the age of seventy-eight, Lossing died at his home in Dover Plains, New York.

Few historians, American or otherwise, can match Benson Lossing in either quantity or quality of output, especially considering his modest educational background. During his fifty-year publishing career, he authored or contributed to over fifty books on American history, geography and biography. Most of his books have been reprinted numerous times over the years, and they continue to remain a staple of bookstores and libraries well into the twenty-first century. Lossing was very much a man of his times, filled with an almost self-righteous pride in his country's accomplishments during both war and peace. But his works also reveal his fondness for the common folk of America—for their stories and experiences—and his wonderful books and drawings have left us with a priceless legacy of our country as it once was.

Michael C. Scoggins
McConnells, South Carolina
September 2004

Preface

On a pleasant morning in June 1848, I journeyed in a light carriage between the villages of Greenwich and Stamford in Connecticut. About five miles from the latter village, the road, by excavation, passed down a steep declivity on a gently inclined plain to the vale a hundred feet below. There I saw, not far from the highway, a flight of rude steps formed of irregular rocks which were almost concealed by shrubbery and brambles. These steps extended from the bottom to the top of the acclivity. A white-haired man stood by a garden gate not far off, of whom I inquired the meaning of the rocky stairway. He pointed to the spire of a church that stood on the elevated plain from which we had just descended, and said:

"Do you see that steeple yonder? Well, before the Revolutionary War the people down here were compelled to go a mile around to get to that church, this hill is so steep; so they made those steps of rocks for their convenience. There's where 'Old Put' came down the steep hill, zig-zag, near them, pursued to its brow by British dragoons who dared not follow him, but sent pistol-balls after him. I was then a stout youngster, and was standing near this very spot when the general rushed by on his powerful horse. I heard him cursing the British between his teeth."

Deeply interested, I said: "Tell me, please, who I am talking to."

"They call me General Mead," he replied.

He was General Ebenezer Mead, of the Connecticut militia, who joined the Continental Army near the close of the Revolutionary War. I made a pencil sketch of the interesting historical locality, thanked the venerable soldier, and, riding on, mused as I traveled.

This incident and its associations made a deep impression on my mind. I had been brought suddenly into the presence of animate and inanimate relics of the old war for independence, both of which were now fading away and soon to be seen no more on the earth, forever. I felt an irrepressible desire to seek and find such mementos of the great conflict for freedom and independence, wherever they might exist, and to snatch their lineaments from the grasp of Decay before it should be too late.

Before I reached Stamford I conceived the plan of a pilgrimage to the dwellings of yet living men and women who were actors in some of the stirring events of the long Past, and to hear from their lips stories of their experience and recollections at the birth-time of our Republic, and to record them for the benefit of posterity.

I returned to New York that evening with my mind full of the project. Before I slept I matured the general plan of a work which should present pictures, by pen and pencil, of objects connected with the old war for independence, historical and personal.

The next morning I marked upon a piece of drawing-paper the size of a page of my proposed book, made upon it some sketches, in sepia, to show the proposed method of illustrating it, and wrote the title-page. With these meagre materials I called upon Messrs. Harper & Brothers—the four founders of the famous publishing house—and before I left them I made arrangements with them to become the publishers of the work. Within a fortnight afterward I was among animate and inanimate relics of the great struggle in Northern New York, which resulted in the capture of Burgoyne and his army at Saratoga.

Such is the genesis of my "Pictorial Field-Book of the Revolution," and such was the beginning of a pilgrimage which occupied many months, and demanded nearly nine thousand miles of travel in the thirteen original States of the Republic and in Canada. This pilgrimage was to the dwellings of living men and women, and to places of historic interest associated with the events which marked the founding of this free and powerful member of the family of nations. Like another old Mortality, I endeavored to deepen the inscriptions which recorded the names and deeds of those who secured our national independence.

From a portion of the abundant store of recorded incidents and delineations of objects then obtained and carefully preserved, which I could not use in detail in my published work, I have drawn the materials for this little volume. The substance of a few of the sketches has appeared in *Harper's Young People*, and one or two other publications.

This volume might have been extended to quadruple its dimensions. In it may be found portraits of some of the men and women whom I visited in their extreme old age forty years ago, and others; with carefully designed representations of a few historical events, in which, as in the portraits, special care has been taken to ensure accuracy of feature and costume.

Benson J. Lossing
The Ridge
November 1888

Hours with the Living Men and Women of the Revolution

A Pilgrimage

Chapter I
The Fifer at Lexington

Lexington! Concord! What American boy or girl, man or woman, has not heard or read of these little Massachusetts villages, where the first earnest blows for American independence were struck and the hot flame of the Revolution first burst out, on April 19th, 1775? Among the first objects of my pilgrimage were these two villages.

It was a charming morning in October 1848, when I traveled by railway from Boston to Concord, seventeen miles northwest of the New England capital. There I spent an hour with Major Barrett[1] and his wife, who "saw the British scamper," and had lived together there almost sixty years. Major Barrett seemed robust at eighty-seven, and his wife, almost as old, seemed as nimble of foot as a matron in middle life. She was a vivacious little woman, well formed, and retained many traces of the beauty of her young womanhood. They had much to tell me of events their eyes had witnessed.

After visiting the place of the skirmish at Concord, I rode in a private vehicle to Lexington, six miles eastward, through a picturesque and fertile country, and entered the famous village at the Green, whereon that skirmish occurred and a commemorative monument now stands. After brief interviews with two or three aged persons there, I drove to the house of Jonathan Harrington, in East Lexington, who, a lad seventeen years old, had heralded the opening of the old war for independence with the shrill notes of the fife.

As I halted before the house of Mr. Harrington, at a little past noon, and saw an old man wielding an axe vigorously in splitting wood in his yard, I entered the gate and introduced myself and my errand. The old man was the venerable fifer.

"Come in and rest yourself," he said kindly, as he led the way into the house.

Although he was then past ninety years of age, he appeared no older than a man of seventy. His form was nearly erect; his voice was firm; his complexion was fair; his placid face was lighted by mild blue eyes, and had but few deep wrinkles; his hair, not all white, was very abundant, and in stature he was of medium height and slender. I took a seat on a chintz-covered lounge, and he sat in a Boston rocking-chair.

"I have come," I said, "to make some inquires about the battle of Lexington."

"It wasn't a battle," he answered; "only a skirmish."

"It was a sharp one," I said.

"Yes, pretty sharp, pretty sharp," he replied thoughtfully. "Eight fine young men out of a hundred were killed; two of them my blood-relations."

"I understand you played the fife on that morning," I said.

"As well as I could," he replied. "I taught myself to play the year before, when the minute-men were training, and I was the only person in Lexington who knew how to fife. That ain't saying much, though, for then there were only eight or ten houses in the village besides the meeting house."

"Did you belong to the minute-men?" I asked.

"I was a minute-*boy*. They asked me to fife, to help Joe Burton make music with his drum for Captain Parker's company. Poor Joe! His drum-head was smashed and he lost a finger in the fight. Captain Amos Parker's company was drilled the night before, for Sol Brown, our nearest neighbor, came from Boston at sunset and said he had seen nine British soldiers walking toward Lexington. Sam Adams and John Hancock were at Parson Clarke's house, where Dorothy Quincy, Hancock's sweetheart, was staying. Gage wanted to catch and hang 'em, and it was believed the soldiers Sol had seen had been sent out to seize 'em that night. A guard of ten men, under Sergeant Monroe (who kept a tavern here), were stationed around

"I taught myself to play the year before, when the minutemen were training."

Parson Clarke's house. At a little past midnight Paul Revere—you've heard of Revere—came riding like mad from Cambridge, his horse all a-foam, for the weather was uncommonly warm. He told Monroe he wanted to see Hancock. 'He didn't want to be disturbed by noise,' said the sergeant. 'Noise!' said Revere; 'you'll have noise enough soon, for the reg'lars are coming.' Hancock heard him, and opening a window called out, 'Revere, I know you; come in.'[2] He went into the house a moment, then came out, mounted his horse, and started on a gallop toward Concord. Very soon everybody in Lexington was astir."

"Were you on duty then?" I inquired.

"No," he said; "I went to bed at eleven o'clock, and, as all boys should do, I slept soundly. My mother, who was a Dunster and one of the most patriotic women who ever lived, called out to me at three o'clock in the morning, 'Jonathan! Jonathan! Get up. The reg'lars are coming and something must be done.' I dressed quickly, slung my light gun over my shoulder, took my fife from a chair, and hurried to the parade near the meeting-house, where about fifty men had gathered, and others were arriving every minute.[3] By four o'clock a hundred men were there. We did not wait long, wondering whether reg'lars were really coming, for a man darted up to Captain Parker and told him that they were close by. The captain immediately ordered Joe to beat the drum, and I fifed with all my might. Alarm-guns were instantly fired to call distant minute-men to duty. Lights were now seen moving in all the houses. Daylight came at half-past four o'clock. Just then the reg'lars, who had heard the drum beat, rushed toward us, and their leader shouted, 'Disperse, you rebels!' We stood still. He repeated the order with an oath, fired his pistol, and ordered his men to shoot. Only a few obeyed. Nobody was hurt, and we supposed their guns were loaded only with powder. We had been ordered not to fire first, and so we stood still. The angry leader of the reg'lars then gave another order for them to fire, when a volley killed or wounded several of our company. Seeing the reg'lars trying to surround us, Captain Parker ordered us to retreat. As we fled some shots were sent back. Joe and I climbed a fence near Parson Clarke's house and took to the woods near by. Climbing over, Joe fell upon a heap of stones

and crushed in his drum-head. His hand was bleeding badly, and he found that a bullet had carried off a part of his little finger. Eight of our men had lost their lives."

"Where were Adams and Hancock all this time?" I inquired.

"Not far off. When the first shots were heard they were advised to fly to a place of safety, for their lives were too valuable to the public to be lost. At first they refused to go, but were finally persuaded, and retired to a thick-wooded hill not far off. Dorothy Quincy went with her lover. They were married in the fall. It is said Sam Adams, hearing of the firing on the Green, exclaimed, 'What a glorious morning for America is this!' I have no doubt he said it, for it was just like him."

"You said two of your blood-relations perished in that fight," I observed.

"Yes," he replied; "they were Jonathan and Caleb Harrington. Caleb and Joe Comes, who lived a mile from Lexington, had gone into the meeting-house to get some powder stored in the loft. They had taken it to the gallery when the British reached the building. They flew to the door, and started on a run for the company. Caleb was shot dead at the west end of the meeting-house, but Joe, though wounded, escaped. Jonathan had stood his ground with the rest. His home was near the meeting-house. He was in front of his own dwelling when the reg'lars fired the third time, when he was shot in the breast and fell. His wife, Ruth, stood looking out of the window with their only child, nine years old, by her side. She saw her husband fall and ran out to help him. He raised up, stretched out his arms toward her, fell again, and was dead before she could reach him. Oh, it was too cruel, too cruel!"

"There were brave men in that little band of patriots," I remarked.

"Brave men!" said the old man, his mild eyes beaming with unusual lustre. "Braver men never lived. Not one of them left his post until Captain Parker, seeing it was useless to fight against so many reg'lars, told them to disperse. There was one man who wouldn't go even then. It was Jonas Parker, of this town. He lived near Parson Clarke's. He had said he would never run from an enemy, and he didn't. He had loaded his musket, put his hat, containing powder, wadding, and bullets, between his feet, and so faced the reg'lars. At the second fire he was wounded and fell on his knees. Then he fired his gun; and though he was dying, he reached for another charge in his hat, when a big red-coat killed him with a bayonet on the very spot where Jonas first stood. Wasn't that pluck?"

"Rare pluck," I answered. "The names of such men should never be forgotten."

"They never will be," replied the venerable patriot excitedly. "Their names are all cut deep in marble on the little monument down yonder on the Green[4]—Robert Monroe, Jonas Parker, Samuel Hadley, Jonathan Harrington, Jr., Isaac Murry, Caleb Harrington, John Brown, and Asahel Porter. Should that marble perish, their names are cut deeper in the memory of Americans."

"You said it was a warm night when Revere rode from Cambridge to Lexington," I remarked.

"Yes, it was a very early spring. Young leaves appeared on the first day of April. The grass on the village Green was so tall on the morning of the 19th that it waved in the light wind that was blowing. At noon that day the quicksilver in Parson Clarke's thermometer rose to eighty-five degrees on the north side of his house, and the door-yards were all bright with dandelions."

"Did you serve in the army afterward?" I inquired.

"No," he said; "father went to the war, and I stayed at home to help mother take care of things, for I was the oldest boy. I played the fife sometimes after that when the young men in the neighborhood were training for the fight."

By his permission, I drew a likeness of Mr. Harrington sitting in his rocking chair, and under it he wrote with a trembling hand, which condition he attributed to the use of the axe that morning,

Jona Harrington
aged 90 the 3d July 1848

His brother Charles, two years younger than he, came in before I had finished the sketch. I could not but look with reverence upon these strong old men, children of one mother, who had borne five sons and three daughters, who had nearly grown to manhood when the war for independence broke out. I bade them farewell, received from the old fifer the benediction, "God bless you," went back to the village Green, sketched the monument, and called upon their kinsman, Abijah Harrington, who was a lad fourteen years old at the time of the skirmish. He saw nearly all of the fight. He had two brothers in it, and had been sent by his mother, trembling on account of her sons, to watch the fray at a safe distance and to obtain information concerning her brave boys. They escaped unhurt.

From Mr. Harrington's I went to the house of Parson Clarke, where I found Mrs. Margaret Chandler, a remarkably intelligent old lady, then eighty-three years of age. She had lived in that house ever since the Revolution; had a clear recollection of events at Lexington on the memorable April morning, and gave me a version of the escape of Adams and Hancock somewhat different from that given by the venerable fifer, but essentially the same.[5]

On the seventy-fifth anniversary (1850) of the conflicts at Lexington and Concord, Mr. Harrington rode in the procession with his brother Charles, aged ninety; Amos Baker, aged ninety-four; Thomas Hill, aged ninety-two, and Dr. Preston, aged eighty-four. At the banquet, after the procession, the aged fifer offered the toast: "The 19th of April, 1775. All who remember that day will support the Constitution of the United States." On that occasion Edward Everett made a speech, in which he remarked that it pleased his heart to see these venerable men beside him, and he was happy to assist Mr. Jonathan Harrington to put on his top-coat a few minutes before. In doing so he was ready to say, with David, "Very pleasant art thou to me, my brother Jonathan."

Mr. Harrington died late in March 1854, when he was almost ninety-six years of age, and was buried with public honors, the highest State officers with a military escort forming a part of the funeral procession.

Chapter II
Independence and the Great Seal

When I was many, very many years younger than I am now, I spent some time with a kinsman in Philadelphia who lived near Independence Square. Near him dwelt two octogenarians, lively relics of our national birth-time, who spent several evenings of each week at the house of my cousin. They were always there together, and the chief burden of their conversation was recollections of their young manhood, and especially of the events of the old war for independence, "a part of which they saw, and a part of which they were."

One of these venerable men was a stout, bald-headed, rotund, jolly old gentleman, and was known by everybody as "Uncle Billy." The other was a tall, spare man, with abundant flowing locks, rather grave and precise in speech, and magisterial in deportment. He was as generally known as "The 'Squire," he having been a justice of the peace several successive years in middle life. Each was more than eighty years of age.

Uncle Billy was the senior of the two by a few months. In his youth he was a clerk with Robert Morris, the patriotic financier of the Continental Congress. Later in life he became a successful merchant, owned a privateer during the second war for independence, and for more than thirty years had lived quietly upon an ample competence in the enjoyment of wife, children, and friends. The 'Squire in his earlier years had been a sort of miscellaneous man—a wit, a scholar to a considerable degree, a journalist, and a great favorite in the best classes of society, and holding some public office now and then. In person he was handsome in form and feature, and a little foppish. He had lived a bachelor, and had saved sufficient money toward the sunset of life to make him comfortable without laboring for it during life's twilight.

The 'Squire was a genius of many features, and had a capacity for many excellent performances. Before his majority he was a sort of sub-editor of *Bradford's Pennsylvania Journal*, and he took pride in pointing to his artistic achievement in engraving, with his penknife, the ugly, disjointed snake representing the English-American colonies, with the significant words below it, "*Join or Die*." It appeared at the head of the *Journal* for many months, to the great annoyance of the King's men, who called it "a scandalous and saucy reflection." The 'Squire became a man-of-all-work—a sort of Caleb Quotem—on Aitkin's *Pennsylvania Magazine* when Thomas Paine was a frequent contributor to its columns.[6]

One evening the 'Squire and Uncle Billy were conversing about journalism in "Revolutionary times," when the former gave a most interesting account of "Tom Paine," as he called him, and his habits. On these occasions I sat like a sponge, absorbing at all points and imbibing an enormous quantity of the "spirit of '76," which affected my life career. The

'Squire said Paine had a remarkable head. His forehead receded very much; his eyes were a sort of steel gray and rather piercing in their glances under excitement; his nose was large and slightly rubicund, and his hair was very dark brown, nearly black. He would come into Aitkin's little back room at the Pope's Head, above the London Coffee House on Market Street, quite early in the morning, chat a little while with any person who might be present, and after he had swallowed his third glass of brandy would take up his pen and begin to write with amazing rapidity. This was a signal for all to leave the room. Paine's pen went on without ceasing, trying to keep up with the rapid pace of his thoughts; and in less than two hours, sometimes, he would finish one of those bold, incisive, logical, and almost fierce essays on the current political topics which appeared from time to time and stirred the hearts of the patriots with holy zeal. Then he would stretch himself out on a settee and sleep soundly for an hour, when he would sally out to meet some congenial friend on the streets or go to some favorite social haunt.

The 'Squire was a sort of Ariel in the public bodies of the city at that time, and his memory being phonographic in its accuracy in reporting sayings and doings, he was held in great repute, and was a favorite at social gatherings. A valued friend of Charles Thomson, the Secretary of the Continental Congress, he learned many a secret motive for acts of that body which were hidden from public ken. The revelations of these things, long years afterward, made the 'Squire one of the most delightful and instructive companions.

One evening I handed to Uncle Billy a document printed and written on parchment and bearing the recumbent seal of the United States, the date as early as 1787. I asked the oracles to explain the origin of the seal, as it seemed to have come down to us in similar form from the beginning of the nation. Uncle Billy handed the document to the 'Squire, saying, "You know more of this than I do; tell the boy all about it." The 'Squire looked at it a moment, and turning to Billy asked:

"Do you remember the fearful thunder-storm that swept over Philadelphia on the evening of July 3d, 1776, and the very cool, bracing wind from the northwest the next morning?"

Uncle Billy answered in the affirmative, and then with much animation he related some of his experience at that eventful time. Morris had sent him to Chester on some business, and the clerk had ridden some distance on the way by the side of an express sent by McKean, a Member of Congress from Delaware, to his colleague, Caesar Rodney. The errand of that express, Uncle Billy said, was of vital importance. The resolution for independence had been adopted on the second day of the month. The preamble, or the declaration of causes which had led to that resolution, had been presented and debated, and there were doubts of its adoption, as there had been developed some strong opposition to it. McKean and Rodney were both in favor of the declaration, but the latter was at his home in Delaware, eighty miles from Philadelphia. McKean sent this express for him. Rodney detained him only long enough for luncheon and to make a change of linen, when he sprang into his saddle, and riding all night (taking a fresh horse at intervals), he reached his seat in (now) Independence Hall in time to cast his vote for the great measure. "So was secured the happy result," Uncle Billy said.

"I was detained at Chester by a shower," said Uncle Billy, "and was compelled to ride all night. I was thinly clad, for the weather had been extremely warm. The sudden fall of the temperature that succeeded the shower was severe upon me, and I was almost frozen when I reached Philadelphia, before sunrise. I observed, as I passed the church of Rev. Doctor

"Rodney detained him only long enough for luncheon and to make a change of linen, when he sprang into his saddle."

Duché, that the electric rods, put up by Doctor Franklin, had been struck and bent by the lightning the previous evening. Pity it hadn't bent the Tory parson back to a good Whig, as he seemed to be when he preached that patriotic sermon in Christ Church, just a year before, to the First Battalion of Philadelphia."[7]

Uncle Billy said Jefferson came into Morris's counting-room that morning, on his way to the State House, and remarked that the mercury had fallen from eighty-nine to sixty-eight degrees in twelve hours.

The 'Squire reminded his companion that it was on that day, with the fresh wind from the north, when Congress so coolly declared the English-American colonies "free and independent States."

"Yes," said Uncle Billy, "I remember the circumstance well. The declaration was debated all the forenoon, and at about two o'clock in the afternoon the final vote was taken. It was supposed that when the great act was accomplished Congress would adjourn for the day. Not so. The grand work was not completed. The representatives of the people had declared the freedom and sovereignty of the colonies, and that they formed a national league of States under one government; it was now necessary that the new government should have an insignia of sovereignty. So, after disposing of some other business. Congress appointed a committee of three members to 'prepare a device for a seal of the United States of America.'"

When Uncle Billy had finished his narrative the 'Squire said:

"Now, let us answer the lad's question about this seal."

"Yes," said Uncle Billy; "the appointment of that committee to devise a seal was about the coolest thing of the day. Why, the bantling was not then four hours old, and nobody felt that it would live; yet they proposed to prepare a coat-of-arms as heavy in weight of sovereignty as was Saul's coat-of-mail in brass. Let me see, who composed the committee?"

"Franklin, Adams, and Jefferson," said the 'Squire, who spoke of Franklin as "one supposed to know everything;" of John Adams as "the plump Bostonian with a bald head," though only forty years of age; and of Jefferson as "that tall bean-stalk, the youngest of the three, who was only two and thirty years of age. But he had a world of book-wisdom under that wiry red hair of his," said the 'Squire.

Uncle Billy remembered hearing Jefferson talking with Morris about the seal a few days afterward, and showing Morris a few weeks later some sketches of a device made by a West India Frenchman named Du Simitere. The 'Squire then remembered that on one hot afternoon Franklin and Adams came into Aitkin's little back room with the French artist, and, using the small table there on which Paine wrote, examined several of his sketches.

"But they came to nothing," said the 'Squire. "The subject was dropped for a while. The war grew hotter and hotter. The members of the committee were engaged at different posts of duty. Other committees were appointed. The subject was briefly considered in Congress from time to time, and new but unsatisfactory devices were presented. It was not until six years after the adoption of the Declaration of Independence that Congress approved a design for the Great Seal of the United State."

"Who did make the approved device of the seal?" asked Uncle Billy, with about as much eagerness as the young listener felt. "Was it not my friend Will Barton, Doctor Ben's younger brother?"

"No, no, Billy," the 'Squire replied, rather impatiently; "he had nothing to do with it until after the whole matter was placed in Secretary Thomson's hands."

The 'Squire went on to say that at about the middle of June 1782, Thomson showed him and Arthur Lee and Elias Boudinot an elaborate device by Barton. It was too elaborate, but in it was a device for the reverse of the seal which pleased them, which was finally chosen for that position. At the same time Thomson showed them a very simple and appropriate device made by an English baronet, and which he had received from John Adams, then the American minister in England. They all agreed that it was the best device yet offered. Thomson reported it to Congress, and it was adopted. "So, you see," said the 'Squire, "we are indebted for our national coat-of-arms—the device on our Great Seal—to a titled aristocrat of the country we were then at war with."

"What was the name of the Englishman?" both Uncle Billy and my kinsman asked, with much eagerness. After giving a minute description of Barton's device, the 'Squire said: "Among others in England who held friendly relations with John Adams was Sir John Prestwich, a baronet of the west of England, who had been a friend of the Americans all through their long quarrel and their struggle with the British Ministry and the Crown. He was an accomplished antiquary. While Adams was conversing with Sir John one day on the bright prospects of the Americans, the former mentioned the fact that his countrymen had not yet adopted a national coat-of-arms. The baronet suggested that an escutcheon bearing thirteen perpendicular bars or stripes, alternate white and red, like those on the American flag, with the chief blue and spangled with thirteen stars, the number of the United States, would make a simple and appropriate device. He further proposed, in order to give it more consequence, to place this escutcheon on the breast of a displayed American eagle, with supporters emblematic of

Great seal of the United States.

self-reliance. Adams was please with Sir John's suggestions, communicated them to his friends in Congress, and the design was approved and adopted. The arms are described in heraldic phrases in the Journals of Congress on June 20th, 1782."[8] Barton's device for the reverse side of a pendant sea was adopted, with some modifications.

Chapter III
The Fair Courier

On a mild, hazy day in January 1849, I was at Orangeburg, S.C., about eighty miles west of Charleston. My purpose was to visit the battle-ground of Eutaw Spring, on the right bank of the Santee River, forty miles distant. I hired a horse and a gig for the journey. The steed was fleet and the road was level and smooth most of the way. It lay through cultivated fields and dark pine forests and across dry swamps, where the Spanish moss hung like trailing banners from the live oak and cypress trees.

At sunset I had travelled thirty miles. I lodged at the house of a planter some distance from Vance's Ferry on the Santee, where I passed the evening with an intelligent and venerable woman (Mrs. Buxton) eighty-four years of age. She was a maiden of seventeen when the armies of Greene and Rawdon made lively times in the region of the Upper Santee, Catawba, Saluda, and Broad rivers. She knew Marion and Sumter and Horry and other less famous partisan leaders, who were frequently at her father's house on the verge of a swamp not far from the high hills of Santee.[9]

"We were Whigs," she said, "but the Tories were so thick and cruel around us when Rawdon was at Camden that father had to pretend to be a King's man to save his life and property. Oh, those terrible times, when one was not sure on going to bed that the house would not be burned before morning!"

"Did you witness any exciting scenes yourself?" I inquired.

"Yes, many. One in particular so stirred my young blood that I actually resolved to put on brother Ben's clothes, take our old fowling-piece, join the 'Swamp Fox,' as the British called Marion, and fight for freedom to call my soul my own."

"What was that event?" I asked.

"You have read, maybe," said Mrs. Buxton, "how Lord Rawdon, after chasing General Greene far toward the Saluda, suddenly turned back, abandoned Fort Ninety-six, in Abbeville District, and retreated toward Charleston. Well, Greene sent Harry Lee with his light-horse to get in front of Rawdon before he should reach the ferry on the Congaree at Camden. He was anxious to call Marion and Sumter to the same point to help Lee. Sumter was then encamped a dozen miles south of our home."

The venerable woman's dark brown eyes sparkled with emotion as she proceeded with the story. She said her cousin, who was on Greene's staff at the time, told her that when the general called for a volunteer messenger to carry a letter to Sumter, not one of the soldiers offered to undertake the perilous task, for the way was swarming with Tories. Greene was perplexed. Brave and pretty Emily Geiger, the young daughter of a German planter in

Fairfield District, had just arrived at the headquarters with important information for the general. She rode a spirited horse with the ease and grace of a dragoon. Emily, aware of the hesitation of the soldiers and Greene's anxiety, earnestly but modestly said to the general, "May I carry the letter?"

Greene was astonished. He was unwilling to expose her to the dangers which he knew awaited any messenger, for the Tories were vigilant.

"They won't hurt a young girl, I am sure, and I know the way," said Emily.

Greene's want was great, and he accepted the proffer of the important service, but with many misgivings. Fearing Emily might lose the letter on the way, he informed her of its contents, that she might deliver the message orally. She mounted her fleet horse, and with the general's blessing and cheered by the admiring officers, she rode off at a brisk gallop. She crossed the Wateree River at Camden Ferry and pressed on toward the high hills of Santee.

"With the general's blessing and cheered by the admiring officers, she rode off at a brisk gallop."

Emily was riding at a rapid pace through an open, dry swamp when one of the Tory scouts, who were on the watch, confronted her with a gleaming bayonet. She reined up her steed. Seizing her bridle-rein, he exclaimed in excited tones, before noticing her face:

"You are my prisoner!"

With perfect composure and in a firm voice she asked:

"By whose authority am I detained?"

The scout was a tall young man, with long flaxen hair flowing from beneath a jaunty slouch hat. He was confounded by the appearance and manner of his prisoner. They had observed a woman riding in apparent haste from the direction of Greene's army toward the camp of Sumter, and suspected her errand. She proved to be a young maiden, fair as a lily, with mild blue eyes and a profusion of brown hair. The young scout, smitten with her beauty and air of innocence, released his hold upon the bridle, when an older companion, made of sterner stuff, seized the reins and led the horse to an unoccupied house on the edge of a swamp and bade her dismount. The younger soldier gallantly assisted her to alight, and she was taken into the house. With proper delicacy the scouts sent for Mrs. Buxton's mother, living a mile distant, to search Emily's person.

"I went with mother," said Mrs. Buxton, "to see a woman prisoner. The door of the house was guarded by the younger scout, who was Peter Simons, son of a neighbor two miles away, and a right gallant young fellow he was. After the war he married my sister, and that youngster who took your horse where you alighted is their grandchild."

"Then you saw the young prisoner?" I asked.

"Yes, and I helped mother search her. We were amazed when we saw, instead of a brazen-faced, middle-aged woman, as we supposed a spy must be, a sweet young girl about my own age, looking as innocent as a pigeon. Our sympathies were with her, but mother performed her duty faithfully. We found nothing on her person that would afford a suspicion that she was a spy. She was released by the scouts, who offered her many apologies for detaining her. She had been too smart for them. While alone in the house guarded by Peter Simons she had eaten up Greene's letter piece by piece. So, secure from detection, she willingly submitted to our search, and told us frankly who she was.

"She had eaten Greene's letter piece by piece."

"'My name is Geiger—Emily Geiger,' she said. 'My father is a planter near Winnsborough, in Fairfield, and I am on my way to visit friends below.'

"Wasn't she smart?" said the old lady. "She *was* going to 'visit friends below'—Sumter and his men—*our* friends likewise, for that matter. When the scouts dismissed her we took her to our house, gave her some refreshments, and urged her to stay with us until morning. But she could not be persuaded, saying the two armies were so near it might soon become impossible to reach her friends. Peter Simons had accompanied us home, and offered to escort Emily to her friends as a protector. She declined his offer, and rode away, bearing our silent blessings. We saw no more of her until after the war."

"Did she reach Sumter's camp in safety?" I inquired.

"Yes, and delivered Greene's message almost word for word as he had written it."

Sumter and Marion joined forces and hastened to Friday's Ferry, at Granby. Rawdon, baffled, did not attempt to cross the Congaree, but fled before the pursuing Americans toward Orangeburg, on the Edisto.

"You say you saw no more of Emily Geiger until some time after the war," I remarked. "What was her fate?"

"A happy one. She had married a rich young planter on the Congaree, named Thurwitz. Soon after the close of the war Emily and her husband, returning from a visit with her parents in Fairfield, went out of their way to revisit the scene of her perilous exploit. They had crossed the Wateree at Camden Ferry, as she had done before, visited the house in which she had been searched, and rode to our home to thank my mother for her kindness on that occasion. They had with them a sweet little baby a few months old. Peter Simons was then my sister's husband and at our house. Emily stood face to face with her jailer for an hour. She freely told her story and owned that she was much startled when Peter seized her bridle, but she controlled her feelings. She told us of her dinner on Greene's despatch, and thought how silly the young scout was in leaving her alone in the house while he guarded the door on the outside. Peter wasn't much of a Tory, and we all rejoiced that a kind Providence had protected Emily from detection.

"The ways of God are mysterious," said the venerable matron, laying her hand on my knee. "Peter's son married Emily's daughter—the sweet little baby she brought to our house—and their son owns a plantation a few miles from here."

Chapter IV
A Lady of Three Manors

My first book was entitled "An Outline History of the Fine Arts," published in 1840 as No. 105 of "Harper's Family Library." It was kindly noticed by the critics, and, encouraged, I felt a strong desire to make a more pretentious effort in the wide and attractive field of historical literature. I had recently read with great interest Freeman Hunt's "Letters About the Hudson," and I conceived the idea of preparing a book, illustrative, by pen and pencil, of the manorial estates on the borders of that beautiful river near which I was born.

The most accessible of these estates from the city of New York, where I then resided, were the Philipse and Van Cortlandt manors. The estate of Philipse, who adhered to the Crown during the Revolution, had been confiscated and sold in parcels by the State. Among the purchasers was Gerard G. Beekman, who bought the first built manor-house, known as "Philipse Castle,"[10] at Tarrytown, and sixteen hundred broad acres around.

Informed that Beekman's aged widow (who was a daughter of Pierre Van Cortlandt, the first lieutenant-governor of the State) was yet living at the "castle," I resolved to make my first historical pilgrimage to her abode. Accordingly, on a pleasant morning late in May 1841, I rode in a light buggy to Tarrytown, then a little village of about one hundred dwelling-houses, twenty-six miles from the city. I dined at one of the two taverns in the village, where I met an old resident who was intimately acquainted with Mrs. Beekman. He kindly offered to accompany me to the "castle" and introduce me to the venerable occupant. After waiting in an anteroom a few minutes we were conducted to a parlor, in which sat in an easy-chair the venerable lady sought. She was dressed in black silk, with a pretty cap partially covering her pure white hair. She did not rise, but received us with great dignity and courtesy. Her voice was strong and musical, her gracious smile was sweet, her deep blue eyes were very animated, though her sight was beginning to fail somewhat, for she was then in the eighty-ninth year of her age, and her whole countenance beamed with intelligence and serene good-humor. She invited us to be seated near her, and when the object of my visit was made known she readily entered into conversation on the subject.

"I have come to you to-day, madam," I said, "chiefly to inquire of whom and where I may obtain trustworthy information concerning the history of the Philipse Manor, or Manor of Philipseburgh; so I will not weary you, but shall be delighted to listen to anything you may be pleased to tell me concerning your long and necessarily eventful experience."

"I am never wearied," she said, "by talking with patient listeners of the long past, for my memory of events of my younger womanhood is so vivid that it requires no mental exertion to recall them."

"How long have you resided here?" I inquired.

"Over fifty years," she replied.

"Did you personally know Mary Philipse, whose charms captivated Colonel Washington?" I inquired.[11]

"Yes, before the war. She married Colonel Roger Morris, of the British army, when I was a little girl, and went to live in their beautiful mansion on Harlem heights."[12] After my marriage my husband and I visited them occasionally. She was the stateliest and most fascinating woman I ever knew. It was well for our country that she did not accept the heart and hand of Washington (if offered), for her imperious will and her power to enslave others by her various charms might have kept him loyal to the Crown."

"Perhaps not," I replied. "His own wonderful will-power may have been too strong for the magic of her fascinations."

"Perhaps so; but he didn't marry her, and all is well," she replied. "I knew her sister Susanna, Mrs. Robinson, well. She was a lovely woman. We exchanged visits occasionally after we occupied our new manor-house near Peekskill. There was a rugged mountain road between us, but we were young and strong and didn't mind the rough journey."

"Then you have occupied two manor-houses?" I remarked.

"Oh, yes, three," she said smiling; "for I was born in the Van Cortlandt Manor-house at Croton, and there passed my infancy and young girlhood until I was married, when I was little more than seventeen years old."

Mrs. Beekman was the second daughter of the "Lord of the Manor" of Van Cortlandt and his wife, Joanna Livingston, and in 1770 she married Gerard G. Beekman and went to New York City to reside. The rising tempest of the Revolution was then shaking the foundations of society. Whigs and Tories were struggling for ascendancy in politics. Her father was an active and uncompromising Whig. She and her husband were in full accord with him. The higher circles of society in which they moved were so imbued with the spirit of Toryism that they retired from the city to her ancestral home near the mouth of the Croton River. There they remained until their own manor-house, two miles northeast of Peekskill, was completed.[13] They first occupied it in 1777, and there they lived during the entire period of the old war for independence, subjected to grievous annoyances and losses at times which were inflicted by Tory marauders who roamed over the neutral ground below, and British invaders occasionally. Her husband was absent from home on public service much of the time, and she was sometimes exposed to insults, depredations, and personal peril; but her courage and fortitude and her bold spirit in emergencies did much to secure her safety.

After the British took possession of Peekskill, in 1777, General Macdougal's advance guard occupied the manor-house and its surroundings.[14]

Mrs. Beekman related to me several stirring events of her life while a resident of the manor-house near Peekskill. She persistently refused to act upon the advice of friends to seek a more assured place of safety back from the riverfront when military operations were active near them. On one occasion she yielded her own judgment to the persuasions of her brother, Colonel Philip Van Cortlandt, when a British scout was abroad from the camp at Verplanck's Point. She took her little family a few miles into the interior, when, after remaining a day and a night, and hearing nothing of the scout, she returned. The marauding troops had visited the manor-house, and, departing, left not a single piece of furniture behind excepting a heavy bedstead. They had plundered the wine-cellar, leaving nothing but empty bottles, and consumed or carried away every particle of food excepting a ham, which hung in a dark part of the cellar. Not a wing of poultry remained but an old rooster, that crowed sturdily on her return. She resolved never to leave her house again in time of danger, and she did not.

Notwithstanding the uniform kindness extended by Mrs. Beekman and her husband to unfortunate enemies who craved assistance, they were sometimes treated with the greatest discourtesy, and even insult and cruelty, by Tory officers claiming to be gentlemen. On one occasion some marauders stole Mrs. Beekman's favorite saddle-horse. The next day young Colonel Samuel Vetch Bayard, one of the most active of the Tory leaders in Westchester County, rode up to the gate of the manor-house on the stolen horse and accosted Mr. Beekman, who was standing near, in an insolent manner. Beekman claimed the horse as the property of his wife and demanded its restoration to its owner.

"Owner!" repeated Bayard, with a sneer. "Hereafter you may look upon your best animals as British artillery horses;" and as he rode away Bayard said:

"I am going to burn the paper-mill of your rebel father;" and he did. The horse was never recovered.

"I never wished Bayard any harm," said the venerable lady, when she related the incident, "but when I heard of his property having been confiscated and that he had fled to Nova Scotia, a fugitive and an outlaw, I didn't grieve. He never returned to his native country."[15]

On another occasion a party of Tories of the better sort in social standing, commanded by Colonels Bayard and Fanning (the latter a son-in-law of Governor Tryon), visited the manor-house and behaved in their usual arrogant manner. One of them insulted Mrs. Beekman by asking:

"Are not you a daughter of that old rebel, Pierre Van Cortlandt?"

With great dignity of manner she replied:

"I am a daughter of Pierre Van Cortlandt, but it is not becoming for one like you to call my father a rebel!" The irritated Tory raised his musket in a menacing manner, when she reproved him most severely for his insolence and bade him leave the house. He was abashed by her courage and the glance of her flashing eyes, and slunk away like a coward, as he was.

Colonel Fanning,[16] who was really a courteous gentleman, soon afterward entered the house and saluted Mrs. Beekman, when presented to her, with great politeness. She told him of the insult she had endured from one of his party. He begged her to accept from him an apology, and promised that not one of them should ever enter her house again.

Mrs. Beekman related a singular incident in her experience which may have had an important bearing on our national history.

One of the most trusted officers on the staff of General Washington at one time was Colonel Samuel B. Webb, father of the late General James Watson Webb, the journalist and diplomat. He had a brother John, who was often an acting staff-officer in the commander-in-chief's military family. He was a lieutenant, and was familiarly known as "Lieutenant Jack." He was a favorite everywhere, and when the American army was operating on the shores of the Hudson River he was a frequent inmate of the Beekman Manor-house. Passing through Peekskill at one time he rode up to the manor-house and requested Mrs. Beekman to take charge of his valise, which contained a new military suit and a considerable amount of money in gold. He was in a hurry and did not dismount, but threw the valise at the feet of Mrs. Beekman at her door, saying:

"Please keep it until I send for it, but do not let anybody have it without a written order from me or brother Sam."

He then rode back to Peekskill and dined. About a fortnight afterward Joshua H. Smith, who lived near Haverstraw, on the west side of the river, and who was acquainted with the Beekmans, rode rapidly up to the manor-house on a bright September day and asked Mr.

Beekman for Lieutenant Jack's valise. Beekman ordered a servant to bring it, when Mrs. Beekman, who had heard the request and the directions to the servant, called out from her room requesting her husband to ask the messenger (whose voice she did not recognize) if he had a written order. On his answering "No" she came from her room. Smith said to Mrs. Beekman:

"Lieutenant Jack had not time to write an order. You know me very well, Mr. Beekman, and when I assure you that Lieutenant Jack sent me for the valise you will not refuse to give it to me, as he is much in want of his uniform."

Rumors had been flying about that Smith, who was quite a prominent character, was not very warmly attached to the Whig cause, and she replied:

"I do know you very well—too well to give you the valise without a written order from Jack or the colonel."

Smith flew into a passion at the insinuation in her answer, appealed to her husband, and urged that his knowledge of the valise being there and that it contained the lieutenant's uniform was sufficient evidence that he was authorized to get it. But Mrs. Beekman persisted in her refusal. She felt an intuitive and indefinable distrust of Smith, and even the expressions of the displeasure of her husband for such treatment of an acquaintance did not move her. Smith rode away as hastily as he came.

It soon came out that Smith had no authority to apply for the valise, and that on that very day Major Andre, the British adjutant-general, was at Smith's house waiting for the evening to start on his return to New York in disguise. As he was about the size of Lieutenant Jack, there can be no reasonable doubt that the suit was intended for his disguise on his return journey through the American lines. The mystery of Smith's knowledge of the valise and its contents was also soon solved. At dinner at Peekskill, on the day when he left the valise at the manor-house, Lieutenant Jack mentioned the fact and nature of its contents. Smith so obtained a knowledge of it. Had he procured the suit André would undoubtedly have escaped and the treason of Arnold been successfully accomplished.[17]

I have mentioned that Mrs. Beekman was kind to her suffering enemies while enduring great wrongs inflicted by them. One day a British officer rode up to her door, dismounted, and inquired for her, and when she appeared he told her he was famishing, and begged for something to appease his appetite. It was just after some plundering British soldiers had stripped her house of food. She left the room, and soon returned with a loaf of bread and a knife.

"Your soldiers have taken every bit of food from me this morning," she said, "all but this loaf; but I will divide it with you. You shall have one half; the remainder I will keep for my family."

Astonished at her Christian charity and generosity, the officer thanked her most cordially, and promised protection to her house in the future.

I tarried nearly two hours with the venerable octogenarian, charmed and edified by her interesting reminiscences. She readily gave me the names of several persons (most of them in the city) who might furnish me with trustworthy information concerning the history and associations of the Philipse Manor.

"This house," said Mrs. Beekman, "is much larger than the 'castle,' occupied by the Philipse family until they built the more spacious lower manor-house at Yonkers. It was called the castle because it was fortified with cannons. The present windows of the cellar under the old part, which were considerably above the ground, were port-holes for the cannon.

"You shall have one half; the remainder I will keep for my family."

There," she said, as she pointed to a small picture hanging on the walls, "is a portrait of the castle as it appeared when he bought it and greatly enlarged the building by additions."

I was permitted to make a pencil sketch of the castle. Near it hung the portrait of a beautiful young woman dressed in the fashion of the period of the Revolution, with hair powdered and curled. It was a picture of the living lady before me, painted soon after the war, when she was a charming matron about thirty years of age. (See page 34.)

"Have you seen the old Sleepy Hollow church?" inquired the venerable woman as I rose to depart.

"I have not," I answered.

"You ought not to return home without visiting it," she said, "for it is a venerable and interesting relic of the past. I could see it from my window were it not for the trees that hide it, for it is only a little way off, close by the highway, where may be seen the bridge over our little Po-can-ti-co, as the Indians called it, where the headless horseman threw his head at Ichabod Crane, as Irving tells us, you know, in his 'Legend of Sleepy Hollow.'"

"I shall certainly visit them before I leave," I replied; and saying farewell to the venerable lady of three manors, I left her presence greatly enriched by the interview. I made my way to the old church and famous bridge. The day was too far spent to allow me to make sketches of them then, and I deferred the task until a future opportunity, which occurred a few years afterward. The church was built in 1699 by Frederick Philipse, the first Lord of the Manor, and his wife, Catharine Van Cortlandt, daughter of Oloff Stevensen Van Cortlandt, the first of the name in America.[18]

This was my first pilgrimage to the famous historic places of our country. The second visit was not undertaken until about ten years afterward. I did not prosecute my cherished plan of visiting and delineating with pen and pencil the manor-houses of the Hudson, for the sufficient reason that I found my purse and my knowledge at that time inadequate to the task.

Nearly six years after this memorable interview Mrs. Beekman died, in the ninety-fifth year of her age. She was of a long-lived race—the Van Corlandts, the Philipses, and the Livingstons. Her father died when he was ninety-four, and her two kinswomen, who were her contemporaries—Susanna and Mary Philipse—died, the former at ninety-four and the latter at ninety-five. The wonderful vigor of her whole being is illustrated by the last act of her life. It is related that a day or two before her death it was necessary to have her signature affixed to an important paper. Supposing she was too feeble to write it, she was told that her simple mark would be sufficient. She asked to be raised in her bed, when, placing her left hand on the fluttering pulse of her right hand, she wrote her name as plainly as in her young womanhood.

Chapter V
Montcalm's Errand-Boy

At noon on a sultry day in July 1848, I arrived at Chambly, an old Canadian village situated at the rapids of the Richelieu or Sorel River, the outlet of Lake Champlain. It was at the time of hay-harvest, and the men and women, boys and girls, were abroad gathering their crops. I was accompanied by a young man, who in a light wagon was conveying me from St. John's, by way of Chambly, to Longueuil, opposite Montreal. My errand at Chambly was to visit and sketch the substantial old fort at the foot of the rapids, about which clustered many stirring memories of the old war for independence. On its site M. Chambly, a French trader from Quebec, built a stockade and gave the name to the hamlet which grew up around it. Having completed my sketch and made a few notes of conversation with an aged resident, we drove to a small tavern by the side of the plank-road leading to Longueuil, a mile distant, and dined.

"Close by that tavern," said my companion, "lives a very old but very smart French blacksmith. I have heard him say that he remembered the great French general Montcalm, and the British general Burgoyne, and other English officers; also the capture of St. John's and Chambly by the Americans. I'll bring him to you if you wish."

"Do so, please," I replied.

As we alighted we saw the venerable man approaching the inn. He was a small, stout-built person, apparently less than seventy years old. His figure was erect, his complexion was a little florid, his blue eyes were bright, his head was covered with plenty of iron-gray hair, and his voice was quick and strong. He came from his forge with his leather apron on, and without coat, jacket, or hat. He could speak very little English, and his French was provincial, but we managed to understand each other. To my inquiries he replied that he was born in Quebec, but when he was a very small boy his mother (a widow) went to Beauport, across the St. Charles, to be housekeeper for Monsieur Bigot, who was living in a fine stone mansion there.

"Will you give me your name?" I asked.

"Certainly; it is François Yest."

"I well remember," said the venerable man, in reply to another question, "when Montcalm, a tall soldier, straight as an arrow, his hair a very little gray, and a scar on one cheek, came to Monsieur Bigot and asked permission to occupy his house as headquarters of the French army for a while. Monsieur Bigot gave him permission. Montcalm had some officers with him, and they occupied a greater part of the house. Mother showed them several rooms, and the general chose for himself one looking out on the Montmorenci

François Yest

road. I was then a little fellow seven or eight years old. At first I was afraid of the soldiers, they looked so fierce and their clothes glittered so. Montcalm patted my head and said:

"'Will you be my boy?'

"'No,' I said; 'I'm mother's boy.'

"Giving me some *bonbons* he said:

"'You'll run for your mother when I want her, won't you?'

"'Oh, yes,' I answered, and from that time until the army went across to Quebec I was Montcalm's errand-boy."

"How long did Montcalm stay at Monsieur Bigot's?" I asked.

"I don't remember. It was very hot weather when he came, and the morning when he left for Quebec with his whole army it was very cold. I think it was in September. The English had got upon the Plains of Abraham, near the city, and Montcalm took his whole army with him to drive them back to their ships, leaving a guard to take care of headquarters."

"You remember the battle on that morning, of course?" I said.

"Oh, yes, and other fighting before it. There had been some hot work at the Montmorenci. It was so near us that the wind, blowing up the river, filled the house with powder-smoke, and many poor wounded Frenchmen were carried by. Not long after Montcalm started for Quebec on that September morning we heard cannons firing and saw the smoke over the city. At a little past noon the French soldiers came flying back to their entrenchments, but the general was not with them. Mother watched and prayed for his return till sundown, when an officer rode up to headquarters and told the commander of the guard that the general had been badly wounded and taken into the city to die. Mother cried all night, and so did I until I went to sleep, for I felt as if I had lost my father again. The general was so good, giving me *bonbons* every day, and patting me on my curly head whenever I did an errand for him. The next morning we heard that the English general, Wolfe, had been killed. General Montcalm died and was buried in Quebec, and we never saw him again. I hear the people there have put up a monument to Wolfe and Montcalm."

"What then became of your mother and yourself?" I asked.

"We stayed with Monsieur Bigot until he died, eleven years afterward, and I had learned the blacksmith's trade. Then we came to Chambly, and with a little money mother had saved we bought a farm of thirty acres, and here I've lived about eighty years. That is my home," pointing to a small whitewashed cottage near by.

"Eighty years!" I exclaimed. "Why, how old are you?"

"Ninety-six and a little over."

"Is it possible!" I said. "You must have witnessed many wonderful scenes hereabout when you were a young man."

"Yes, indeed I have. I was working our farm and following my trade when the Bostonians came down the river and besieged St. John's. We French people were friendly to the Bostonians, for we did not like to live under the English any more than they did. Men came among us to recruit, and many joined the invading army. I would have done so, but mother was old and sick, and I could not leave her; but I helped the Bostonians all I could. We wanted them to take Fort Chambly, in which Carleton had left only a small garrison. We knew its capture would hasten the surrender of St. John's and Montreal, and so we hoped to get rid of English rule. We had formed a plan for its capture, and one night late in October I met some scouts to whom I described our plan. They took me to the tent of a Major Livingston, and I told him all.[19] The next day three detachments were prepared for a rapid march. They arrived near Chambly toward midnight. We had put artillery on *bateaux*, and on these the heavy guns were taken to the head of the rapids, where they were mounted on carriages and drawn to the point of attack before daylight. This was our plan, and it worked well. After very little fighting the strong fort was surrendered, with all its heavy cannons, ammunition, and stores, and these were used in carrying on the siege of St. John's. It, too, was surrendered a few days afterward, and very soon the English scampered away from Montreal."

"Why didn't you Canadians stick to the Bostonians throughout the war?" I inquired.

"Because they insulted us Catholics, and General Arnold cheated us," was the brief and eminently truthful reply.

"We were made to believe that they were no better than the English, if as good," he continued. "Our recruits left them, and they got no more, and when the Bostonians were driven out of Canada the next summer we believed they would never whip the English, and we Canadians, having friends with the actual masters of Canada, though we had no love for them."

"And so you helped the English as you had helped the Bostonians?"

"Yes, and more. When Burgoyne came up the Sorel we helped him get his cannons and stores above the rapids, and the next year I helped to furnish stores for his army encamped at St. John's, preparing to go on that campaign into New York, in which he lost his army and was made prisoner."

"You saw Burgoyne?"

"Yes, many times. He was a large man, fifty years old, I should think. He was proud, but kind-hearted. In his army were many Canadians, and a host of Germans formed a part of his forces.[20] They were rough-looking fellows, and in their camps they made the air blue with smoke from their pipes. I shod six of the general's horses one day, and he praised my work. Not long afterward he sent for me, and handing me half a crown he said:

"'Here, my boy' (he called me boy, though I was twenty-five years of age—I suppose because I was so small), 'that's for information you gave of the rebels last night.' I had told the guard at our outposts that a large scouting party of Bostonians were near. Burgoyne was a magnificent man."

The chatty old blacksmith would have talked on all day, and told me more things worth knowing, I believe; but time was precious, and I could not listen longer. I was permitted to make a pencil portrait of him as he sat in a chair. He did not comprehend what I was doing until I showed him the drawing. When he saw that it was a picture of himself he laughed like a pleased child. I thanked him for coming to the tavern and telling me so much that I was glad to hear, and putting a coin in his hand bade him adieu. As he was about to leave, my young companion, wishing to please him, offered to "treat" him to a draught of brandy and water. The old man's eyes lighted with indignation, for he regarded the kindly meant offer as a wicked temptation for him to violate the temperance pledge which he had signed, for the first time in his life, the year before.

"No," he said firmly; "you cannot tempt me to break my work. I promised I'd never drink any more liquor, and I never will. I'm obliged to you, but I will never do it."

He had reached the door when he uttered the last brave words. I took his hand and said:

"You are a courageous and faithful soldier among these enemies," pointing to the decanters and bottles filled with the ammunition of the destroyer. "You won't desert your post. Tell me, please, about your signing the pledge."

"You see," said the old man, the tears filling his eyes, "my wife—blessed woman—died about five years ago. Then I had no one to help me remember. I was so sad that I was ready to do anything that promised to cure the heartache."

"'Take rum or brandy; it will soothe your feeling and make you happy,' said a neighbor, who drank a little everyday. I had been a temperate man all my life, and did not fear the temptation. I took a little brandy every day. It always revived my spirits. I wanted more and more. It soon became my master. One day good Father Pequit took me by the hand and said: "'François, you are in danger of becoming a drunkard, and so disgracing your children.'

"The last words went like a dagger to my heart. 'How can I help it?' I asked, almost in despair.

"'Sign the temperance pledge and heed it,' said the good father.

"'I will!' I earnestly cried, for the suggestion gave me hope.

"Father Pequit brought the pledge to me an hour afterward, and on the smooth face of my anvil I wrote upon it the name of FRANÇOIS YEST. Then I gave a blow to the paper with my sledge-hammer to seal it. I'll never break that seal—never, never! I tell everybody to sign the pledge. It is a grand barricade against the tempter."

This stanch apostle of temperance began his ministry at the age of almost ninety-five years! Small in stature, he nevertheless seemed to loom up before me a stalwart hero, a moral knight panoplied in invulnerable steel. I again pressed with deep reverence the labor-hardened hand of François Yest, Montcalm's errand-boy.

"Then I gave a blow to the paper with my sledge-hammer to seal it."

Chapter VI
The Patriotic Widow of the Congaree

I was at Fort Motte station, near the Congaree River, in South Carolina, not far from the junction of that stream with the Wateree, on a bright, frosty morning in January 1849.

"Will you direct me to the Fort Motte plantation?" I said to a lad.

Pointing up a gentle slope, he said:

"On the top o' the hill is Mr. Love's house, which they call Fort Motte. It is only a short walk from here up that dirt road."

At the summit I found a very aged man, with thin white hair and warmly clad, sitting upon a log by the wayside. He was resting his hands upon a long staff, and smiled pleasantly as I approached. After a cordial greeting I asked:

"Is that Fort Motte?" pointing toward a rather fine-looking house for the region, standing on the high rolling plain which sloped to the swamps on every side.

"So they call it," said the old man; "but it ain't the fort we tuck from the British more'n sixty year ago—burnt 'em out, you may say."

"Were you one of its captors?" I asked.

"I reckon I wuz," replied the old man. "D'ye see that scar?" pointing to his forearm, which he had bared of its sleeve. "A red-coat's bullet made it in a scrimmage afore the siege. I was Horry's leftenant. Horry, you know, wuz Marion's right-hand man when hunting Tories. He stuttered when hurried to say anything quick. Coming suddenly on a Tory camp one night, he wanted to tell us to fire quick. He said: 'Fi-fi-fi-fi—*shoot*, darn ye!' and we blazed away in the dark."

"Why was this called Fort Motte?" I inquired.

"Bless your soul!" said the old soldier, with animation. "Don't you know Becky Motte—Becky Brewton that wuz—lived here? Mighty plucky woman wuz Becky Motte. A purty woman, too; as purty as a pictur, though she wuz well-nigh forty year old, and had a darter married to Gineral Pinckney, who wuz then a prisoner in the hands of the Britishers. She wuz a Charleston lady, daughter of a Britisher, and this wuz her best country house—a might healthy place on this hill. The British druv Becky out of her house, dug a big ditch all around it, piled up a high bank o' dirt 'round the ditch, next the house, and so made a fort of it—a purty strong fort agin muskets and rifles. It was a nice house, but not so fine as Mr. Love's, which Becky built right away after the war. I helped draw timber to build it."

"The British drove Mrs. Motte and her family out of her house, did they? Where did they go?" I asked.

"To her overseer's, on yon hill," he replied. "Becky wuz a rich widder; lost her husband early in the war, and lived here in the summer. At that farm-house she showed raal grit, I tell ye; grit that made us all feel as if we would willingly die for her—yes, *die* for her."

"How did she show grit?" I asked, as I seated myself on the log beside the veteran in the bright sunshine.

"Well, you see," said the old patriot, as his voice waxed stronger by the stimulus of vivid recollections, "they had her house, and five hundred red-coats were in and around it.[21]

Rebecca Motte

Leftenant-Colonel Lee—Legion Harry, you know—you must have heard of him—a dashing young trooper then of my age—twenty-five—had joined us with his light-horsemen, and we all pushed forward, horse and foot, for this place to drive off the Britishers. That very mornin' some troopers from Charleston came to the fort with despatches for Lord Rawdon at Camden. They were about to leave when we appeared at Becky's farm-house. They wuz skeered and didn't go. Lee had a little six-pounder cannon, which he placed in battery on the knoll you see yonder, speckled with the stumps of some trees lately cut down. The red-coats had no artillery, so we had 'em, we reckoned."

"Who were Lee's troopers?" I asked.

"Mostly young Virginians, I reckon, ready to go where he might lead; and he wuz ready to lead where he might lead; and he wuz ready to lead wherever his country needed brave men. He wuz a handsome young man, with large, dark eyes and brown hair. The gay uniform of his men made the homespun clothes of Marion's brigade appear meaner than ever. But we had the grit as well as they."

"How did you take the fort with only that little fieldpiece?" I inquired.

"I'll tell ye. Lee dismounted his troopers, led 'em into a narrow hollow up to a short way from the fort, and with the help of some niggers began to dig toward it, and threw up breastworks while we took post at the fieldpiece to defend it in case the red-coats should come out and attack us. They were ordered to surrender. They said they wouldn't. Jist then we heard that Rawdon wuz retreating from Camden and had sent troops to join the garrison at Fort Motte. That very night their campfires were seen on a hill not far away. The sight made us lively, I tell you. Something must be done quickly. To batter down their works with our baby cannon or reach them by digging trenches would take too much time. But Lee was up to anything. 'We must burn 'em out,' he said.

"The shingles on the house wuz dry as tinder, for the sunshine wuz hot on that day, at the middle of May. 'I can send fire on 'em with arrows,' said Lee, 'and they'll blaze in a minute.' But he didn't like to do it. Becky Motte wuz his friend; her son-in-law wuz his friend; but he thought of his country first and his friends afterward. When he mentioned it to Becky, the plucky woman clapped her hands and said, 'Good! good! Do it if you can. Burn the house if they won't surrender.' Wasn't that real grit—real patriotism?

"Lee sent another order for the red-coats to surrender. They knew help was nigh, and they wouldn't do it. He asked Marion, 'Have you a man who can shoot straight with a bow and arrow?' 'Yes,' the general said; 'Nathan Savage is as good a shot as any Indian.'

"A bow and arrow were quickly made and taken to Lee's headquarters at the overseer's house, with Nathan. He tried the bow and said, 'It ain't strong enough.' 'Here, darter,' said Becky to the youngest, who married Colonel Alston, 'run and git the Indian bow and arrows.'[22] Turpentine torches were fastened to two or three of the arrows, when Nathe sent them like blazin' stars straight to the roof. The shingles smoked, and we hurrahed. They blazed, and we shouted. The red-coats ran up and began to knock off the burning shingles. Shots from the six-pounder raked the loft and sent the Britishers scampering pell-mell below. Pretty soon a white flag was seen waving, and at noon we had 'em; the red-coats were all our prisoners. Wuzn't we happy fellers! I didn't mind the bullet-hole in my arm a bit just then. Becky Motte—plucky Becky Motte—wuz as happy as any of us, though her fine house wuz in ruins. She invited the British officers, as well as ours, to her farmhouse to lunch, and, perfect lady as she wuz everywhere, she wuz as purlite to her country's enemies as to its friends.

"Nathan Savage is as good a shot as any Indian."

"While we were at table," continued the old soldier, "word came to our gineral that some of his men wuz amusing themselves by hanging Tories. Marion hurried out, and with his drawn sword ran to the spot in time to save the life of one of 'em. It wuz Tom Cunningham, one of the worst, who died at Kingston last year. The gineral threatened to kill any man who should attempt to harm another prisoner. A just man, a brave man, a Christian man wuz Gineral Marion."

When the venerable soldier had finished his story I strolled on to the house of Mr. Love, where I spent several hours very pleasantly. He said the narrator was a worthy pensioner and a man of truth, and that the traditions of the country as well as official reports were in general agreement with his story of the capture of Fort Motte by Lee and Marion. I wrote the name of the venerable pensioner on a scrap of paper, soon lost it, and have been unable to recall it.

The remains of the entrenchment around the house were still quite prominent at the time of my visit.

While I was in Charleston, not long afterward, I had a pleasant interview of almost an hour with a venerable lady (Mrs. Bristow), whose mother was a distant kinswoman of Mrs. Motte. When I spoke of my recent visit to the scene of her noble act of patriotism, the face of the aged matron lighted up with emotion, for slumbering memories of the past were awakened. She gave me an account of several pleasing incidents in the life of the patriotic widow of the Congaree.

"I knew Rebecca Motte well," said the old lady. "Her house, one of the finest in the city, was only a few doors from my father's dwelling. I was a girl fourteen years old when her country house was destroyed. When, in the spring of the year before, the British took possession of the city, I remember seeing a swarm of red-coats at her house. British officers had taken possession of it for headquarters. But she, brave woman that she was, refused to leave the house, but presided at her own table every day, whereat sat many British officers. At first, my mother told me, they were frequently very rude in their remarks about the 'rebels' in her presence. She often retorted boldly and keenly, but always with great dignity, and she soon won their admiration for her unflinching courage, her calm self-possession, her mental superiority, and her many charms of person and character."

It is related that the cultivated British officers sought the society of this brilliant widow because of her entertaining conversation, though often compelled to wince under her polished sarcasm.

After the destruction of her mansion near the Congaree, Mrs. Motte returned to her home in Charleston. General Green was then driving the British forces from the upper country toward the sea. On being inquired of at Charleston by a British officer concerning news from the country, Mrs. Motte replied:

"All nature smiles, for everything is Greene down to Monk's Corner"—a few miles from Charleston. For this remark she was banished from the city for a very brief period.

Chapter VII
The Cicerone at Ticonderoga

At the old Lake House, at the head of Lake George, long before the spacious Fort William Henry caravansery was built, I became acquainted with a charming young woman and her brother, from the vicinity of the lofty Kaatsbergs fringing the Hudson Valley. They were making a brief pleasure tour. A sudden tempest of wind, rain, and lightning had kept us all within the parlors during a sultry evening in July 1848, and there the acquaintance began. We voyaged down the lake together the next morning in bright sunshine and invigorating air.

The young lady was a model tourist—intelligent, sensible, vivacious, and enthusiastic. With her brother she had encamped among the charcoal-burners of the Kaatsbergs, hunted in the mountains, and fished for days in the glens, and was a favorite companion of Thomas Cole, the artist, in his sketching excursions. While others were afraid of spoiling their complexions in the sunlight or of crumpling their smooth dresses or soiling their fine bonnets and gloves, she bade defiance to dust and crowds, for her brown linen sacque, with its spacious pockets for a guide-book and other accessories; her lisle-thread gloves, her jaunty sun-hat, and her free but sweet and modest demeanor toward all gave herself and brother no uneasiness. And when, at the foot of the lake, I climbed to the lofty and broad seat of the driver of an old-fashioned stagecoach, for a ride of four miles through a most picturesque region, to Ticonderoga, on Lake Champlain, she too sprang up, as nimble as a squirrel, to the notable perch of observation for a traveler. As we journeyed among the hills, caught glimpses of the Green Mountains, and heard droll stories of his experience from the lips of our Jehu of slow speech, her ringing laughter awoke responsive echoes.

A glance, from our seat, of the gray old ruins of Fort Ticonderoga, as we drew near the Pavilion on the lakeshore, made us as impatient as children to be among them. With these pleasant companions, and alone, I spent hours among the remains of the old fortress, listening to the stories of a venerable soldier, who, in body, haunted the place in the pleasant summer-time. We were about to send to the Pavilion for a guide and an interpreter of the mysteries around us, when this white-haired man, supported by a rude staff, came from the ruins of the northern line of barracks and offered his services. They were accepted, and after my companions for a day had departed down the lake for Quebec I sat at the foot of one of the crumbling walls and listened to the old man's interesting stories. His name was Isaac Rice; his age was eighty-five; no kindred of his was left on the earth; by a technical error he lost a just title to a pension for military services in the Revolution and, he was obtaining a precarious support from the free-will offerings of summer visitors for whom he acts as cicerone.

Though feeble in body, his mind appeared clear and vigorous.

"Did you assist in the capture of this fort?" I inquired.

"No," he replied, "but my oldest brother did. I was then nearly thirteen years old. When Burgoyne took the fort I was a drummer-boy of the garrison that escaped, and I saw the British general deliver his sword to our General Gates three months afterward. My brother was twenty years old on the day when the fort was taken. We lived near the old Catamount Tavern, in Vermont—did you ever hear of it?—where Ethan Allen lived a long time, and where the Green Mountain Boys were mustered in the troublesome times before the Revolutionary War.[23] I've heard my brother tell many things about the taking of the fort on that morning."

"Didn't they get into the fort by a covert way?" I asked.

"Yes; and there's where it was," he said, pointing to a hollow among a mass of stones and earth. "My brother, who was a sergeant, led a squad of men just behind Colonels Allen and Arnold."

"Arnold—Benedict Arnold?" I said inquiringly.

"Yes. Arnold joined the Vermonters and others at Castleton on the evening before the capture." The veteran then told the story clearly as his brother had related it to him. Arnold came without officers or troops—only one servant. He introduced himself to Colonels Allen and Easton—Easton of Pittsfield—and taking from his pocket a commission as colonel issued by the Massachusetts Committee of Safety, he claimed the right to command the whole force gathered there for the expedition. Allen disputed the claim. Arnold persisted, when the indignant Green Mountain Boys declared that only Colonel Allen should lead them, or they would shoulder their muskets and go home.

Arnold was compelled to yield, and all prepared to cross the narrow lake that night. Boats were scarce, and only about eighty men were enabled to cross over. Allen took with him Nathan Beman, a farmer's boy, who had been much at the fort and knew all about it. At daybreak they were ready to climb the bank to the sally-port of the fort, when Arnold again claimed the right to command. Allen disputed his claim. Arnold swore he *would* command. Allen swore he shouldn't. This quarrel was in undertones, so as not to be heard by the sentinels above. The men interfered, and it was arranged that Allen and Arnold should enter side by side, Allen on the right as commander. Then they all moved to the sally-port at the covert way, led by Allen and Arnold. The sentinel snapped his fusee and ran into the fort, followed by the Americans close upon his heels; and before the garrison could spring from their pallets and seize their arms the invaders had possession of the parade within the fort and took them all prisoners as they came out. Young Beman then led Allen up a rickety stairway to the apartments of Captain De Laplace, the commander. Knocking loudly on the door with his sword-hilt, he commanded the captain, in a stern voice, to appear instantly or the garrison would perish. At that moment De Laplace, who had been awakened by the commotion on the parade, clad only in shirt and drawers, sprang to the door, the frightened face of his pretty little wife appearing over his shoulder.

"Surrender!" shouted Allen.

They were old acquaintances.

"By what authority do *you* command me to surrender this fort?" said De Laplace indignantly.

"In the name of the Great Jehovah and the Continental Congress!" thundered Allen, raising his sword over the captain's head.

De Laplace began to speak, when Allen shouted, "Silence!" The commander obeyed, and an unconditional surrender followed.

"You said you were a drummer-boy here when Burgoyne took the fort?"

"Yes," replied the veteran; "I was then a lusty lad nearly thirteen years old. My brother was one of the garrison."

"And so you became well acquainted with every part of the fort, I suppose. Will you point out the principal localities?" I asked.

"Yonder," said the guide, pointing toward the best-preserved line of the barracks, built of stone, two stories in height, and forming a quadrangle, "were the officers' quarters. A wooden balcony extended along the second story, which was reached by a flight of stairs. The first door in the second story, on the left, was the entrance to the commandant's apartments. Between the ruined wall on the extreme left is seen Mount Defiance, on which Burgoyne erected a battery. Come with me and I will show you the bakery."

The aged cicerone took me to the southeast angle of the fort. Near it was an underground room twelve feet wide and thirty feet long arched with bricks, with a ruined fireplace and chimney at one end. On each side of the fireplace was an oven ten feet deep. On the right was a window and a door opening toward the water.

For more than half a century the walls of the fort had been the common spoil for all who chose to avail themselves of such a convenient quarry. These ruins presented a most attractive object to the tourist and the historical student.

"When Burgoyne came up the lake, you left Ticonderoga in a hurry, didn't you?" I inquired.

"Not exactly," said the veteran. "General St. Clair felt strong enough to defend the fort against an expected direct assault, and would not listen to a demand to surrender; but when, in the course of a few days, it was found that the British had planted a battery of heavy guns on the mountain yonder—Mount Defiance—from which they could send plunging shot into the fort, the general chose the latter way, and at midnight on July 5th, 6th, we left the fort as silently as possible, the bulk of the garrison crossing over to Mount Independence, yonder, and marching rapidly toward Skenesborough, now Whitehall. At the same time

"In the name of the great Jehovah and the Continental Congress!" thundered Allen.

about two hundred *bateaux*, laden with baggage, ammunition, and stores, guarded by armed galleys, were sent up the lake toward the same place. We were pursued in Vermont by the British, and were overtaken among the hills at Hubbardton, where we were compelled to fight, and were dispersed. The flotilla was also pursued and was destroyed. Many of St. Clair's men finally joined General Schuyler at Fort Edward. My brother was slightly wounded in his leg at Hubbardton, and a bullet took off one of my fingers, as you see, and made a hole in my drumhead."

"You say you saw General Burgoyne surrender his sword to General Gates?"

"I did, and felt very happy," said the old man.

"Did that surrender take place when the British army laid down their weapons on the flat at Saratoga, near the river?" I asked.

"No," said the guide. "When the arms were all laid down, General Burgoyne and his principal officers rode toward General Gates's headquarters. They were met by Gates and his staff at the head of his camp, where the officers of both armies were introduced to each other. Burgoyne wore a rich coat of scarlet and gold. Gates wore a modest blue frock-coat. The whole party then went to headquarters and dined. After dinner the American troops were drawn up in two lines, between which the British army passed, escorted by cavalry with the American flag, and a band of music playing 'Yankee Doodle.' Then the two generals came out of Gates's *marquee* and faced the halted procession. Gates wore his best regimentals. Then Burgoyne stepped back a pace and presented his sword to Gates before the two armies. Gates bowed, took the sword, and immediately handed it back to Burgoyne. Then the British army filed off and started for Boston to embark for home. I was a drummer in the escorting band, and stood not more than three rods from the generals. Burgoyne was a large, stately man; Gates, who was about the same age, was smaller and less dignified in appearance and manner."

The sun was now passing behind the great hill on which the British planted their menacing cannon, and named the eminence in consequence "Mount Defiance." As the aged cicerone sat leaning against a ruined wall I made a pencil sketch of his form and features, under which, with a trembling hand, he wrote his name and age.

As we walked slowly together toward the Pavilion in the evening twilight, I inquired of my venerable instructor if he was in the military service of our country after the surrender of Burgoyne.

"For a while," he answered. "I enlisted as a private in a company of which my brother was captain, and was stationed in Eastern Massachusetts. We went with General Sullivan to Rhode Island to drive the British away, and were in a battle on Quaker Hill. My father, an aged man, dying in the spring of 1779, I left the army and went back to Vermont to manage our little farm for my mother. Misfortune overtook us, and we lost the land. I had married, but had no children. My wife died, and I have been alone in the world ever since, laboring with my hands for daily bread. The good Lord is kind to me, for I have never been seriously sick in my life. I believe He will take care of me to the end, which cannot be far off."

Chapter VIII
The Child Captive of Wyoming

At three o'clock on a cool September morning in 1848 I left Easton, Pa., on a stage-coach for the Wyoming Valley, sixty miles distant. Although there were only three other passengers—two women and a baby—I took a seat with the driver, for there were promises of a pleasant day-dawn and magnificent scenery. But when we had ascended to Nazareth, chilling vapors that came up from the river and valleys caused me to seek comfort within the coach. We passed through the Wind Gap and breakfasted at the Roscommon Tavern. Then I resumed my seat with the driver. At noon we reached the gently undulating summit of the Pocono Mountains, and dined at John Smith's, two thousand feet above tide-level.

For about twenty miles we rode over that dreary waste, where, here and there, a lofty pine, a tamarack, or a less ambitious cedar rose from a green sea of shrub-oaks. Here the gray eagle wheeled undisturbed, the bear made his lair, and wild deer roamed in abundance. The wind blew cold from the northwest, and I was happy when we reached the brow of the Wilkesbarre Mountain, a little before sunset, and began to descend into the warmer atmosphere of the charming Wyoming Valley that spread out in enchanting beauty far below us. I can never forget the right royal supper at the Phoenix Hotel, by the side of the beautiful Susquehanna, that appeased a voracious appetite after a sixty-mile ride in healthful mountain air—venison steak and cranberry sauce, warm biscuits and honey!

Early the next morning I started on a pilgrimage to places and persons identified with the stirring scenes enacted in the Wyoming Valley in the summer of 1778. I first visited Mr. Charles Miner, the early historian of the valley, who, with his blind daughter, blessed with a remarkable memory, heard the fearful and pathetic story from the lips of more than forty intelligent survivors of the work of desolation. I then called on the venerable Mrs. Myers, near Kingston, a living witness of the woes of Wyoming, who was then eighty-seven years of age, totally blind, but exceedingly cheerful and kindly communicative. She was the last survivor of the inmates of Forty Fort,[24] when it was besieged and captured by the Tory leader, Colonel Butler, and his Indian allies. She possessed the little round table on which the treaty, at the time of the surrender, was signed. I found the venerable woman seated in an easy-chair, peeling apples. She received me with great dignity and kind courtesy, and entertained me for an hour with reminiscences of her girlhood experience amid the exciting scenes of the Vale of Wyoming.

Mrs. Myers, *née* Bennett, was sixteen years old at the time of the memorable invasion of the valley, and was in Forty Fort when it was surrendered. She remembered every minute occurrence there with perfect clearness. She remained two weeks in the valley after the surrender. The Indians kept her face painted black and a white fillet around her head as a protection against the tomahawks of strange savages, and she was treated very kindly by them. After the barbarians, white and red, had left the valley, she returned, with her family, and had enjoyed for seventy years the sweets of peace and domestic happiness.

"I am like a withered stalk whose flower hath fallen," said the venerable lady; "but," she added, with a pleasant smile, "the fragrance still lingers. Have you see Joseph Slocum?" she inquired.

"I have not even heard of him," I replied.

"You ought not to leave the valley without seeing him," she said, "for he can give you a more interesting story about the events I have been relating to you than any other living person—the story of the captivity of his little sister, and the discovery of her sixty years afterward. He lives not far from the hotel."

I passed several hours of that day with Lord Butler, a grandson of the leader of the band of patriots who gallantly opposed the Tory and Indian invaders of the valley. He kindly accompanied me to the most interesting localities in the neighborhood—Forty Fort, the monument, the chief battle-ground, Monocacy Island, Wintermoot's Fort,[25]etc., and I spent the evening pleasantly and profitably with the venerable Joseph Slocum, whose family was among the sufferers in the Wyoming Valley. He gave me a minute account of the capture of his little sister Frances by the barbarians, and the final discovery of her.

Mr. Slocum's father was a Friend, or Quaker, and was distinguished for his kindness to the Indians. He remained unharmed at the time of the invasion, and his dwelling was untouched by incendiary fire. But his son Giles was in the battle. This, doubtless, excited the ire of the Indians, and they resolved on vengeance. Late in the autumn they were seen prowling about the house, which was not far from Wilkesbarre Fort. A neighbor had been made a prisoner, and his wife and two sons found a welcome home in the Slocum family. One morning the two boys were grinding a knife near the house, when a rifle-shot and a shriek brought Mrs. Slocum to the door. An Indian was scalping the eldest boy, a lad of fourteen. The barbarian rushed into the house and seized a little son of Mrs. Slocum. The frightened mother exclaimed:

"See! He can do thee no good; he is lame!"

The Indian released the boy, and taking the daughter Frances gently in his arms, seized the younger of the two boys outside, and hastened to the mountains. Mrs. Slocum's little daughter, nine years old, caught up Joseph (my informant), who was two and a half years old, and fled in safety to the fort, when an alarm was given but the barbarians were beyond successful pursuit. They also carried off a black girl, seventeen years of age.

About six weeks after this event Mr. Slocum and his father-in-law were shot and scalped by prowling Indians while foddering cattle near the house. The savages escaped with their horrid trophies.[26] Mrs. Slocum, bereft of father, husband, and child, and stripped of all possessions except the house that sheltered her, could not leave the valley, for nine helpless children were yet in her household. She trusted in the God of Elijah, and if she was not fed by the ravens she was spared from the vultures. She mourned not for the dead, for they were at rest; but little Frances, her lost darling, where was she? The lamp of hope was kept burning, but years rolled by and no tidings of the little one came. When peace returned and friendly intercourse with Canada was established, two of the little captive's brothers started in quest of her. They traversed the wilderness to Fort Niagara, on the border, offering rewards for her discovery, but in vain. They returned, convinced that the child was dead.

"And taking her daughter Frances gently in his arms, seized the younger of the two boys outside, and hastened to the mountains."

But the mother's heart was still not in the grave. Her embodied spirit seemed to hold communion with that of her child, and she often said:

"I know Frances is living. Something tells me that she is alive and well."

At length the mother's heart was cheered. A woman (many years had now passed, and Frances, if living, must be a full-grown woman) was found among the Indians who answered the description of the lost one. She only remembered being carried away from the Susquehanna. Mrs. Slocum took her home and cherished her with a mother's tenderness. Yet the mysterious link of sympathy that binds the maternal nature to its offspring was unfelt, and the bereaved mother was bereaved still.

"It may be Frances, yet it does not seem so. Yet the comer shall be welcome," said Mrs. Slocum. The foundling felt no filial yearnings, and both being convinced that no consanguinity existed, the orphan returned to her Indian friends. From time to time the hope of the mother would be refreshed, and journeys were made to distant Indian settlements in search of the lost sister, but in vain. The mother was finally laid in the grave, and little Frances was almost forgotten.

The brothers of the child-captive had become aged men, and their grandchildren were playing upon the very spot from whence Frances was taken. In the summer of 1837, fifty-nine years after her capture, intelligence of Frances was received. Colonel Ewing, an Indian agent and trader, in a letter written at Logansport, Ind., to the editor of the Lancaster (Pa.) *Intelligencer*, gave such information that all doubts about her identity were removed. She had told Mr. Ewing that her name was Slocum; that her father was a Quaker, and that she was taken from near the Susquehanna River when she was very young. The letter came to the knowledge of Joseph Slocum, when he and his sister who carried him to the fort journeyed to Ohio, where they were joined by their younger brother, Isaac. They proceeded to Logansport, where they saw Mr. Ewing and ascertained that the woman he had written about lived twelve miles from the village. She was immediately sent for, and toward evening the next day she came into the town, riding a spirited young horse, accompanied by her two daughters, dressed in full Indian costume, and the husband of one of them. An interpreter was procured (for she could not speak a word of English), and she listened seriously to what her brothers had to say. She answered but little, and at sunset departed for her home, promising to return the next morning. The brothers and sister were quite sure it was Frances, though in her face nothing but Indian lineaments were seen, her color alone revealing her origin.

"True to her appointment," said Mr. Slocum, "she appeared the next morning, accompanied as before. I mentioned a mark of recognition which my mother had said would be a sure test. One day, while playing with a hammer in a blacksmith shop, when I was about two and a half years old, I gave Frances a blow upon the middle finger of her left hand which crushed the bone and deprived the finger of its nail. This test I withheld until others should fail. When I mentioned it the good woman was greatly agitated, and while tears filled the furrows of her aged face she held out the disfigured finger, but said nothing. There was no longer any doubt that we had found our lost sister, and a scene of deep interest ensued. Her affections for her kindred which had slumbered more than half a century were aroused, and she made earnest inquiries after her father, brothers, and sisters. She opened her full heart to us and gave us a history of her life.

"'The Indians when they took me from the house,' she said, 'went to a rocky cave in the mountains. They were Delawares. The next morning they departed for the Indian country.

That first night was the unhappiest of my life; but I was kindly treated and was carried tenderly in their arms when I was weary. I was adopted in an Indian family and brought up as their daughter. I soon almost forgot my mother. For years I lived a roving life, and liked it. I was taught the use of the bow and arrow, and became expert as a hunter and in all out-of-door exercises. When I was grown to womanhood both of my Indian parents died, and I soon afterward married a young chief of the nation and removed to the Ohio country. I was treated with more respect than even the Indian women generally. I was taught to ride on horseback, and was not required to cultivate the soil or bear burdens. I always remembered my carrying off; and so happy was I in my domestic relations that the chance

Frances Slocum

of being discovered and compelled to return among the white people was the greatest evil that I feared. For I had been taught that the white people were the implacable enemies of the Indians, whom I loved. My husband died, and my people having joined the Miamis, I went with them, and married one of that tribe. I have children and grandchildren, and am very happy.'

"When she had concluded her narrative, she lifted her right hand in a solemn manner and said:

"'And this is as true as that there is a Great Spirit in the heavens!'"

Her second husband had been dead many years. She was entirely ignorant of her native language. She had received the name of *Ma-con-a-qua*, or "A Young Bear," and was a pagan endued with a Christian spirit.

On the day after the second interview the brother and sister, with the interpreter, rode out to the home of the found captive. Her dwelling was a well-built log-house in the midst of cultivation. A large heard of cattle and sixty horses were grazing in the pastures. Everything betokened plenty and comfort, for she was wealthy when her wants and her means were compared. Her annuity from the Government, which she received as one of the Miami tribe, had been saved, and she had about one thousand dollars in specie. Her white friends tarried with her several days, and not long after their return home Joseph and his daughter, the wife of the Hon. Ziba Bennett, of Wyoming, again visited her and bade her the last farewell. On that occasion she was induced to sit for her portrait to an artist named Winter, residing at Logansport, whom I met at Lafayette, Ind., in 1860. It was half-length life size. At the time of my visit it was hanging in Mr. Slocum's parlor, and I was permitted to make a pencil copy of it. The costume was very simple—an underdress of scarlet and a mantle of black cloth, with a large flowing sleeve on one side.

Frances Slocum—*Ma-con-a-qua*—the Child Captive of the Wyoming Valley, died in 1844, and was buried with considerable pomp, for she was regarded as a queen among her tribe. When the Miamis were removed from Indiana, the "lost sister" and her Indian relatives were exempted. The affecting story of her life was laid before Congress, as eloquently did John Quincy Adams plead her cause that he drew tears from the eyes of many members. Congress gave her a tract of land a mile square, to be held in perpetuity by her descendents, and there her children and grandchildren were living at the time of my visit in the Valley of Wyoming.

Chapter IX
The Last of Sumter's Men

It was a dreary day in January 1849, when at three o'clock in the afternoon I arrived at Mr. Leslie's plantation, within two miles of King's Mountain battleground in South Carolina. I had traveled with a single horse and light wagon the rough road that skirted the foot of King's Mountain. The heavens were shrouded with clouds, and snow which had fallen during the night and mingled with mud more than fetlock deep had jaded my horse. I explained to Mr. Leslie the object of my journey, expressed a desire to visit the battleground of King's Mountain that afternoon, and asked him to show me the way, it being only two miles from his house.

"Your beast is tired," said Mr. Leslie. "I have two good saddle-horses in the stable."

They were brought out. We rode to the famous field, among wooded gravel hills, viewed the topography of that strange battleground, made two or three sketches, and returned at twilight. The venerable William McElwees, Mr. Leslie's father-in-law, had just arrived. He was a stout-built man, of medium stature, with an unmistakable Scotch face, flowing white hair, blue eyes, and, though eighty-seven years old, seemed about as vigorous in mind and body as a hale man at sixty. He was the last known survivor of General Sumter's famous partisan band in the old war for independence. His reminiscences formed the theme of the evening's conversation.

"When and where did you join Sumter?" I inquired.

"Just before Clinton took Charleston and Cornwallis began to overrun the State in 1780. South Carolinians were discouraged, and hundreds took British protection. Sumter would not yield, but retired into North Carolina. I followed him. There he gathered a little band of exiles, and we returned. Sumter called for recruits. Very few came until after we struck the camp of the wicked Tory Chris Huck on a hot night in July. We killed the leader and scattered his followers to the wind.[27] Huck was a profane and profligate wretch. He hated Presbyterians intensely; murdered one of them while on his way to a place of worship on a Sunday with a Bible in his hand, and burned a minister's house. When we struck Huck he had about two hundred mounted men. Our party numbered only one hundred and thirty-three all told. Timid men now took courage and joined Sumter's standard. Governor Rutledge made him a brigadier, and I was commissioned a lieutenant."

"You were engaged in some stirring events afterward," I said.

"Indeed I was. We struck British and Tory parties here and there so unexpectedly and sharply that Cornwallis declared Sumter was his greatest plague in the Carolinas. They called him 'The South Carolina Game Cock.'

"Before the end of July our little army numbered about six hundred and was daily increasing. Sumter felt strong, and he determined to attack a British and Tory force about two hundred and fifty strong, at Rocky Mount, near the Catawba. They occupied log-houses at the foot of the slope, which were surrounded by *abatis*, as the French call it—a row of felled trees laid brush-end forward. We had no cannons, so we got to the top of the hill, filled an old wagon with dry brush and straw, fired it, and sent the hissing mass down the slope against the houses. The British, seeing the peril, hoisted a white flag. At that moment a shower of rain put out the fire, and the little garrison defied us. We could do nothing, so we withdrew, crossed the Catawba, and pushed on toward Hanging Rock." [28]

"What caused your defeat there?" I asked.

"Rum, sir!" said the old soldier emphatically—"rum, the deadliest enemy of mankind. You see, we had whipped the British and Tories completely and sent them running like frightened deers, leaving their camp and all behind. Their camp was tempting, and our men, instead of pursuing, engaged in plundering. They drank freely of the liquors found in the officers' quarters. Our force became disordered, and when the British rallied and returned two thirds of our men were too drunk to do duty. With about two hundred men our brave leader charged upon the enemy, but seeing a reinforcement for them coming, we retreated with some prisoners and booty."

"You were hard pushed at Fishing Creek,"[29] I remarked.

"Indeed we were—surprised—badly surprised."

"I thought Sumter was always wide-awake," I said.

"So he was, but 'accidents will happen in the best of families,' you know. Sumter had been sent by Gates to intercept a British escort from Ninety-six. We captured more than forty wagons loaded with clothing and stores, and were returning to the Wateree when we heard of the defeat of Gates near Camden. So we went up the river to Fishing Creek. We did not dream that an enemy was near. At noon on a hot August day, while our arms were stacked, the horses were grazing, and more than half the men were asleep under the trees, the fiery Tarleton with his cavalry dashed among us, seized our arms and horses, killed about one hundred and fifty of our men, and made three hundred prisoners. Sumter, who seemed never to sleep, seeing his men slaughtered and dispersed, sprang upon his big white horse, and closely followed by myself and a drummer-boy with his drum, on one bay mare, fled into North Carolina, nor stopped until we reached Charlotte. We made a sorry figure when we rode into the village. Sumter was without a hat, I without a coat, and the drummer-boy, sitting astride behind me, had only a shirt on, having just come out of the creek, where he had been bathing. Our horses were without saddles."

"What then?" I asked.

"Action! Only Marion was then in the field with Whigs in South Carolina. Sumter went immediately to the upper country, where a few of his men who had escaped joined him, and many volunteers flocked to his standard. We were then all mounted, and were soon joined by other parties. We had an opportunity presently to show Tarleton that Americans could strike heavy blows as well as British. Late in November he chased us. We had encamped at Blackstocks, on the Tiger River, in Union District, where Tarleton overtook us with a part of his force. We fought desperately, and at dusk we set Tarleton and his men running for life and liberty, leaving about two hundred of his men on the field, nearly one hundred of them dead."

"I have heard there were many brave women in that region," I observed.

"Brave! Why, they helped the cause almost as much as the men! There were Grace and Rachel Martin, Mrs. Dilland, Dicey Langston, and scores of others in that lonely country left at home by the men in arms, and they performed their part in the contest nobly, I assure you. Grace and Rachel were the young wives of two sons of the Widow Martin, of Ninety-six District, who were in Greene's army. These young women were with their mother-in-law. One evening they were informed that a British courier, with two guards, would pass that way with important dispatches for a British post beyond. They put on their husbands' clothes, provided themselves with arms, and lay in ambush by the side of the wood. Late in the evening the courier and his escort came along, when the young women suddenly sprang before them, presented their weapons, and bade the travelers surrender with their paper. Utterly surprised, they obeyed, and were paroled. Returning, they stopped at Mrs. Martin's and craved accommodation for the night. On being asked why they had returned so soon, they said they had been made prisoners by two lads, and showed their parole. The young women allowed their captive guests to depart the next morning in ignorance that their captors had entertained them. The dispatches were sent to Greene."

"Who was Dicey Langston?" I inquired.

"A girl as brave and patriotic as Joan of Arc, and not so old—only fifteen or sixteen. She was the daughter of a Whig in Laurens District, whose son was in my company in Sumter's army. She was continually getting valuable information about the movements of the Tories and giving it to the Whigs. At one time she heard that Cunningham and his 'Bloody Scout' were about to attack a settlement in which her near relatives resided; she determined to give them warning. Leaving her home at near midnight, she sped through swamps and thickets and across running streams until she reached the Tiger River. It was swollen, rendering the ford dangerous. She pushed into the river in the darkness, and in the channel, neck deep, she became confused. But she gained the shore, gave the warning, and when the scout came the inhabitants had fled to a place of safety.

"One day she was captured by some Tories and ordered to give some information about a Whig neighborhood from which she had come. She positively refused. The leader, placing a pistol at her breast, said, 'Tell, or you shall die in your tracks.'

"Dicey snatched off a long kerchief which covered her neck and bosom, and said:

"'Shoot me, if you dare!'

"He was about to fire, when a companion threw up his hand and saved the brave girl's life. I might tell you a hundred stories of the actions of our brave women, but it is getting late."

"Tell me, please," I said, "where were you at the battle of King's Mountain?"

"In it," he promptly replied. "I was at home on furlough, and volunteered to resist Ferguson and his Tories. We met him among the gravel hills you saw today. He was killed, and a large portion of his men were made prisoners. You saw the stone that marks the spot where Ferguson fell and was buried, did you not?"

"Yes," I replied, "and made this sketch of it," handing him my drawing.

"On that limb," said Mr. McElwees, pointing to one on the tree nearest the memorial stone given in the sketch, "I saw ten Tories hung. They were a murderous gang and deserved their fate."

"Did you see Sumter after the war?" I inquired.

"Often. He died only about twenty years ago, when he was almost a hundred years old. I was at his funeral at his home, South Mount, near Camden."

Turning to a grandchild, Mr. McElwees said, "It's nine o'clock; please hand me a Bible." He read a short chapter, then a hymn was sung, and he concluded the simple family worship with a most impressive prayer.

I bade the venerable man goodnight with feelings of gratitude for a rich entertainment.

"Shoot me, if you dare!"

Chapter X
Flora Macdonald

In the winter of 1849 I started to follow the line of General Greene's famous retreat before Cornwallis from the Catawba to the Dan, in 1781; but soon turned eastward to Fayetteville, N.C., where I arrived toward sunset on a mild January day. In the evening I called upon Mrs. McL—, a sprightly Scotchwoman and a widow, eighty-seven years of age. She was the "oldest inhabitant" in all the region. She had been brought from Scotland when she was an infant. I was told that she well remembered the notable Flora Macdonald when that lady was a resident of North Carolina.[30] She received me very kindly, and seemed to be pleased to be questioned about the famous heroine of the Hebrides.

"I was a girl of fourteen," said Mrs. McL—, "when Flora and her husband came to Cross Creek [the old name of Fayetteville]. She was then about fifty years of age, not very tall, but a very handsome and very dignified woman, with fair complexion, sparkling blue eyes, the finest teeth I ever saw, and hair nearly covered with a lace cap and slightly streaked with white. She had endured much trouble. Her voice was sweet music," continued Mrs. McL—, "and oh, how the poor and the church missed her when she went home, after experiencing much trouble here! She was often at my mother's house when she first came, and I almost worshipped her because of her beauty and goodness."

Flora Macdonald

"Is her dwelling-place here yet standing?" I inquired.

"No; it was partly burned in a great fire here about twenty years ago. As you pass from the market-house to the court-house you may see the ruins of it near the creek."

The old lady then stepped to a quaint-looking chest of drawers, and taking out a dingy letter written by Flora to Mrs. McL—'s elder sister, then a maiden of twenty, handed it to me to read. It was a brief note, but an exceedingly interesting one, as it was in bold handwriting of the heroine of Skye. I was permitted to make a copy of it and a tracing of Flora's signature. Here is a copy:

February 1, 1776.

DEAR MAGGIE: Allan leaves to-morrow to join Donald's standard at Cross Creek, an' I shall be alone wi' my three bairns. Canna ye com' an' stay wi' me awhile? There are troublesome times ahead, I ween. God will keep the right. I hope a' our ain are i' the right, prays your guid friend,

FLORY MACDONALD.

"You see," said Mrs. McL—, "she wrote her name Flory—she always did.[31] The letter was written at her new house at Cameron Hill, near the Barbacue Church, where the good Mr. Campbell preached as often as possible. Flora was a pious member of the Barbacue congregation."

"Then she did not live here long?" I said.

"No; she soon moved to Cameron Hill, about twenty miles north of here."

On the day when that note was written the royal Governor of North Carolina issued a proclamation calling upon all friends of the King to assemble with arms at Cross Creek and join his standard. The Macdonalds were all stanch loyalists. They had been loyal to the Stuarts, now they were loyal to the House of Hanover.

The troubles of Flora in North Carolina now began. Her husband and others, to the number of about fifteen hundred, mostly Scotchmen, readily obeyed the call of the governor.

"Flora came with her friends," said Mrs. McL—. "I remember seeing her riding along the line on a large white horse and encouraging her countrymen to be faithful to the King. Why, she looked like a queen. But she went no farther than here, and when they marched away she returned to her home. She dined with us, and the next day sister Maggie went out to Barbacue to stay awhile with Mrs. Macdonald, as she had desired."

Nearly a month afterward these Scotch loyalists were routed, dispersed, made prisoners, or killed in battle at Moore's Creek Bridge. Flora's husband was among the prisoners, and was sent to Halifax Jail. He was soon afterward released on parole, when he left North Carolina with his family for Scotland, in a British war-sloop. On the way the vessel was attacked by a French cruiser, when the courage of the English seamen and marines appeared to desert them, and capture seemed inevitable. They were about to surrender when Flora appeared on deck, and by words and deeds so stimulated their spirits that they beat off the enemy, and the Macdonalds were landed safely on the soil of the Isle of Skye. During the engagement Flora was severely wounded in the hand. She remarked, when speaking of her peculiar situation, "I have hazarded my life for the House of Stuart and the House of Hanover, and I do not see that I am a great gainer by it."

Flora Macdonald was the mother of five sons and two daughters. She retained much of her beauty and all of her loveliness of character and dignity until the last. She was always modest, always kind, always sweet and benevolent in disposition. She died early in March 1790, and was buried in the cemetery at Kilmuir, in the Isle of Skye. Her shroud, as she had requested long before her death, was made of the sheets on which the Young Pretender, whom she helped escape to France, reposed at the house of her kinsman, the Laird of Kingsburgh, on the night before he sailed for the continent. Two years later the remains of her husband were laid by her side. Their resting place was covered with greensward for eighty years. In 1871 a beautiful monument was erected over them.

"When the news of Flora Macdonald's death came to the Barbacue congregation," said Mrs. McL—, "a solemn funeral service was held in the church, when the Rev. Dr. Hall preached a sermon."

The venerable lady attempted to tell the story of Flora's exploit which made her famous, but her narrative was so mixed and meager that it was unsatisfactory. I will endeavor to give the narrative as concisely and clearly as possible from the best authorities, prefacing the story with the remark that I regard my personal interview with one who had conversed with the heroine as a memorable privilege. I gratefully pressed the hand of the old lady when I bade her goodbye.

The "Young Pretender," as Prince Charles Edward Stuart, grandson of James II of England, was called, had landed in Scotland to attempt the recovery of the British throne, from which his grandfather had been driven nearly sixty years before. He drew hosts of adherents around him. He fought battles with the English, but was finally beaten at Culloden. His followers were dispersed, and he was for five months a fugitive, hunted from mountain and glen, from crag to cave, among the highlands of Scotland. He at length found a hiding place on the Isle of Uist, one of the Hebrides, and a friend in Laird Macdonald.

To the house of this laird came his young kinswoman Flora, in June 1746, a beautiful and romantic girl, fresh from school at Edinburgh, to visit her relatives. The island was swarming with soldiers in search of the prince, at the head of whom was Flora's stepfather. The fugitive could not much longer elude his pursuers. Lady Macdonald had conceived a plan for his escape, but found no assistant willing to brave the consequences. Flora heard the plan and became deeply interested. She had seen the prince when he and his followers rode into Edinburgh.

"Will you undertake to assist the prince, Flora?" asked Lady Macdonald.

"I will," was the prompt reply.

She was joined in the perilous enterprise by a young kinsman, Neill Macdonald. Flora obtained from her stepfather a passport from the island, with Neill and three others as a boat's crew, and Betsy Burke, a stout Irish woman, whom she pretended to have engaged as a seamstress for her mother in the Isle of Skye.

Betsy Burke was the prince in disguise. On a bright afternoon the little party embarked from Uist. A terrific storm burst upon them that night, but they reached Skye in safety the next morning. Confronted by soldiers on shore, they rowed eastward and landed near the home of Sir Alexander Macdonald. Leaving the prince among the rocks, Flora told her secret to Lady Macdonald, who entertained them all for the night.

On the following morning Flora accompanied the prince to Portree. She had conducted him as her servant through crowds of soldiers and people who were eagerly seeking him, for a reward of $150,000 had been offered for his arrest. A small vessel was at Portree ready to convey the fugitive out upon the free ocean and bear him to the friendly coast of France. She bade him adieu. The prince kissed her and said:

"Gentle, faithful maiden, I entertain the hope that we shall yet meet in the royal palace."

"Gentle, faithful maiden, I entertain the hope that we shall yet meet in the royal palace."

They never met again. Neill Macdonald accompanied the prince to France, where he married and settled at Sancerre, the place of long residence of some of the clan Macdonald who accompanied King James to the continent. His son, born there four years before the birth of Napoleon Bonaparte, became the great military leader, the eminent Marshal Macdonald.

Flora's complicity in the escape of the prince became known, and she was taken to London with Macdonald of Kingsburgh and others, and cast into the Tower as a prisoner of State. When George II asked her sternly, "How could you dare to succor the enemy of my crown and kingdom?" she replied, with sweet simplicity, "It was no more than I would have done for your Majesty had you been in his place."

Her romantic story touched the best hearts of England with sympathy and admiration. It was so evident that Flora was not a partisan of the Young Pretender nor of his religious faith, and that she had acted from the generous and benevolent impulses of a woman's heart, that she and her kindred were pardoned and released. The house wherein she tarried, a few days afterward, was crowded with the nobility and gentry of both sexes, who congratulated her upon her freedom and poured money into her lap. Her extreme youth and radiant beauty captivated all hearts. A chaise and four horses were provided by Lady Primrose to convey her back to her home; and so the fair young girl who went to London to be hanged as a felon returned in state, followed by the blessings of thousands.

Four years after her release Flora married Allan Macdonald, the son of the Laird of Kingsburgh, and not long afterward she became the mistress of the mansion wherein Prince Charles slept in the Isle of Skye on the night before his escape to sea. There in 1773 she entertained Dr. Johnson and his shadow, Boswell, and allowed them to occupy the same room, and Johnson the same bed in which the prince slept. Although she had then been a wife more than twenty years and the mother of several children, Dr. Johnson spoke of her as a woman of pleasing person and elegant behavior.[32] Her husband was then in embarrassed circumstances, and they contemplated going to join their countrymen, who had emigrated in large numbers to North Carolina. Thither they went in 1774, but failed to find the coveted repose, as we have observed, and they returned to Scotland and their beloved Skye.

Chapter XI
The Last Survivor of Washington's Life Guard

"The third time always conquers," declares a "wise saying." I found it verified in my attempts to obtain an interview with the latest-known survivor of the famous corps known as "Washington's Life Guard," which was formed, in the spring of 1776, of trustworthy men of the Continental Army, for the protection of the person, papers, and baggage of the commander-in-chief. Of this corps the unfortunate martyr, Nathan Hale, was an original member. It consisted of one hundred and eighty picked men from different regiments. Its first commander was Caleb Gibbs, of Rhode Island.

A new organization of the Guard occurred at Morristown, N.J., at the close of the spring of 1777, when its numbers were increased and a part of the Guard were mounted as cavalry. Washington required these men to be, in stature, not more than five feet ten inches, nor less than five feet nine inches—"sober, young, active, and well-made." Gibbs was yet their commander. He was succeeded near the close of 1779 by William Colfax, of New Jersey, the grandfather of the late Vice President of the United States, Schuyler Colfax.

The uniform of the corps consisted of a blue coat with white facings, white waistcoat and breeches, black stock and black half-gaiters, and cocked hat with a blue and white plume. Their flag was of white silk, on which was painted one of the Guard holding a horse, and in the act of receiving a banner from the Genius of Liberty, personified as a woman leaning upon the Union shield, near which was the American Eagle. Upon a ribbon was the motto of the corps—CONQUER OR DIE. This flag (which I have seen and sketched) was made after the national banner of the United States—the Stars and Stripes were adopted in June 1777.

Informed that Sergeant Uzal Knapp, the probable last survivor of Washington's Life Guard, and Major Robert Burnet, one of the general's escort into the city of New York on the morning when the British evacuated it in November 1783, were living not far from Newburgh, on the Hudson, I made three attempts to visit them. The first effort was a failure; at the second I had a brief interview with Major Burnet, and the last resulted in an interesting conversation with both of the veterans, on a pleasant September afternoon. I rode first to the residence of Major Burnet, whom I had visited on a hot evening in August. Approaching his house by a green lane, shaded by ancient willows planted by his own hand, I greeted the old patriot as he sat in his armchair just inside the wide open front door of the spacious entrance hall of his dwelling. Seated there, I was entertained for an hour by his reminiscences of the old war for independence. He gave me a graphic account of the great meeting of officers at the Temple, on the campgrounds of the Continental Army, not far from Newburgh, where, in a dignified address, Washington gave a scathing rebuke of the unpatriotic and seditious spirit manifested by the famous "Newburgh Letters," in the spring of 1783, which were the occasion of the assemblage.

"Washington entered the Temple unattended, after the officers were seated," said Major Burnet; "took a seat at one end of the long room, and in a few minutes he rose with a paper in his hand. Taking from his waistcoat pocket a pair of silver-framed spectacles, he said, in his usual deliberate manner of speaking, as he placed them before his eyes, 'You see, gentlemen, that I have not only grown gray but blind in your service.' These words powerfully touched every heart, and from that moment every soul in the room was loyal to the chief and the cause."

Major Burnet's father was a Scotchman, and his mother was a native of Ireland. He was a lieutenant of artillery, and was in charge of a battery at West Point at the time of the discovery of Arnold's treachery. He was afterward promoted to major, and was one of the officers delegated to attend the meeting at the Temple just alluded to. He continued in the army under the immediate command of Washington, and was one of the founders of the Society of the Cincinnati. When the Americans marched into the city of New York, accompanied by Washington, on the day of the British evacuation, he commanded the rear-guard. He was also present at the final parting of Washington with his officers at Fraunce's Tavern in Broad Street.

Major Burnet was eighty-seven years of age. He had seen what few men in modern times had beheld—namely, the living representatives of seven generations of his kindred.

Sergeant Knapp lived a short distance from Major Burnet. Where we were in conversation, the venerable sergeant, Burnet's senior in age, rode by at a brisk pace, homeward. The major said, with a trace of jealousy in his tone, "See how carelessly that man rides; he will have a fall yet that will kill him. I ride as well as he, but more carefully."

I bade Major Burnet farewell, and arrived at the house of

"You see, gentlemen, that I have not only grown gray but blind in your service."

Sergeant Knapp just as he had alighted from his horse. He left the steed in care of a laborer and invited me into his dwelling. I felt sure that he could tell me more about events at Washington's headquarters at New Windsor than any other living person, and with very little preface, after we were seated, I asked:

"Were you with Washington all the time that he was at New Windsor?"

"Certainly," he replied; "I was one of the Guard, and I believe I am the only one living."

"When did you join the Guard?" I asked.

"Not long after the battle of Monmouth Court-house," he replied. "I joined the army when I was eighteen, and my first battle was at White Plains. I was afterward with General Wooster in the affair at Ridgefield, in Connecticut, where he was killed. Then I joined the light infantry under Lafayette, fought in the battle at Monmouth Court-house, in New Jersey, on that terribly hot Sunday in June, and was chosen a member of the commander-in-chief's Guard a month afterward."

"Where did Washington reside at New Windsor?" I inquired.

"In a plain, old-fashioned Dutch farmhouse, built by the father of Simeon De Witt," he answered. "It was not large, but comfortable in cold weather," he continued, "and there General and Lady Washington lived and entertained company from some days before Christmas in 1780 until the spring of 1781. That house stood in the village, and was pulled down many years ago. Great officers of the army with their wives were entertained there, and there were lively times there on the Christmas after Lady Washington came."

"How were the Guard housed that winter?" I asked.

"First in tents and then in huts," he replied. "The weather was very mild. The river did not freeze up at Newburgh until after New Year. The bay was as clear of ice as in May. The water guard boats could go and come as they pleased. Why, only a few days before Christmas Washington ordered Colonel Humphreys to take as many of the water-guard as he might think necessary and attempt to bring off the Hessian General Knyphausen from Morris's house, on the upper part of York Island, or General Clinton from the city. Humphreys went with two whale-boats and a barge, and twenty-five or thirty men, including officers, but did not succeed, owing to the high winds."

"You say General and Mrs. Washington gave entertainments occasionally. Were you ever at headquarters at such times?" I asked.

"Always, as special guard at the door of the house, or on other duty there. I shall never forget the Christmas dinner at headquarters, a few days after Lady Washington came."

"Why do you call her *Lady* Washington?" I inquired.

"We soldiers always called her so. She was a real lady, if there ever was one," he answered.

"Well, as I was saying," continued the veteran, "it was Lady Washington's first entertainment there. There was trouble at that time in getting poultry for headquarters, particularly turkeys, for the camp had lately been established, and the farmers in all direction had been robbed of their fowls by the bad soldiers. As I knew all the farmers in the neighborhood, I was sent to procure poultry for this occasion. I had traveled far without success, when I called at the house of General James Clinton, who was then in the Northern Department. His wife Molly, one of the best of women, had locked up several turkeys for her family's use, but gladly let me have three of them for the general, with which I returned to headquarters."

"Who were at that Christmas dinner?" I inquired.

"I cannot remember all," he replied. Sitting in silence for a while in summoning memory to the front, he said:

"There were two young French officers from Rochambeau's army at Newport; Governor George Clinton and his wife or daughter; some gentlemen and their wives from the neighborhood; Molly Clinton (who, you know, was the mother of De Witt Clinton), and the staff-officers, two of the them with their wives. Colonel Hamilton, Washington's secretary, was at Albany, where he had married General Schuyler's daughter only ten days before, and did not return until after the holidays. There were about twenty at the table, which was set in the biggest room in the house. Besides poultry, there was beef and mutton. After dinner spiced wine was passed round, followed by pies, puddings, apples, nuts, and cider. I was detailed, as a sergeant, to take charge of the Guard Band, which played lively tunes during the feast; and so I saw all that was going on in the room, for we were stationed in the passage through which each guest went to the dining-room.

"On such occasions Colonel Hamilton generally sat at the head of the table, but now being absent, the general presided at one end of the table himself, and Lady Washington at the other end. She was a short, stout-built, and good little woman. We all loved her. Before the guests sat down, the general, standing, asked a blessing with solemn tones and closed eyes. Old Billy, Washington's body-servant, whose head appeared like a bunch of white sheep's wool, was the chief waiter on that occasion, and moved with great dignity.[33] In the evening some of the young people of the village were invited in, particularly in dancing, until nine o'clock, when the company broke up. Captain Colfax, who commanded the Guard, was a guest at the dinner. We all had a good time."

Sergeant Knapp gave me many other interesting reminiscences of his life as a guardsman, and I lingered until the sun had set and the twilight was fast deepening. I bade the venerable patriot farewell, and he said:

"Oh, I forgot to tell you the best part of the story of the Christmas dinner at headquarters. There was a pretty and proud little girl in the village, named Anna Brewster, then in her teens, but less than three feet high. She refused Lady Washington's invitation to the dinner because she supposed it was given only to gratify the curiosity of the other guests. She soon found out her mistake, for Lady Washington called at her mother's house, and little Anna was afterward very often at headquarters. When she grew to full womanhood she was only a yard high. She lived a maiden until she was seventy-five years old, and then died. Perfect in form, sweet in temper, she was beloved by everybody. Anna Brewster was the smallest woman in America."

It was dark when I left the old guardsman's door, and I rode back to Newburgh in the light of a full moon. I met Sergeant Knapp once afterward. It was at a celebration at Newburgh of an historical event. There was a civic and military procession. I was invited to ride in a barouche with Sergeant Knapp and the orator of the day. The sergeant and I were invited guests. He had a conspicuous seat on the platform, and when the orator had finished his address I was invited to introduce the venerable guardsman to the people. The audience testified their respect and reverence for the hero by hurrahs which almost brought echoes from Beacon Hill and the Storm King, looming up from the Hudson not far off, on the crests of which Sergeant Knapp had seen signal fires blazing during the old war for independence. And when, an hour later, this last survivor of Washington's Life Guard arose at the public banquet to depart, with a solemn but firm voice he invited the whole company to his funeral. Just four months to a day from that time, when he was little past ninety-six years of age, his spirit took its flight, and many who were at the feast were mourners at the burial. His remains were interred near the tall flag-staff at Washington's headquarters at Newburgh. Over them stands a chaste mausoleum of brown sandstone, fashioned by the eminent sculptor, the late Henry K. Brown. It was erected by Company F, Nineteenth Regiment Newburgh Guards, in the early summer of 1860.

Chapter XII
"Mother Bailey," and Two Wars for Independence

In the early autumn of 1848 I sojourned a few days at New London, on the Thames, in Connecticut, and visited places of interest in the vicinity. Pre-eminent among these was Mount Ledyard, or Groton Heights, on the opposite side of the river, which is surmounted by a tall granite obelisk one hundred and twenty-seven feet high. It was erected in 1830 near the dilapidated old Fort Griswold, then without ordnance or garrison, to commemorate the deeds of brave patriots who perished there in a brutal massacre, while helpless prisoners, by British and German soldiers, led by a New Jersey Tory, in September, 1781.

I crossed the Thames on a bright morning, and was climbing the hill on which the monument stands, when I met an old resident of Groton, a little village opposite New London. He was a small boy when the massacre occurred, and remembered it, but could give very little information. He referred me to "Mother Bailey," the postmistress at Groton, who was a young woman at the time, and whose lover, who became her husband, narrowly escaped.

After visiting the fort and monument I called upon Mrs. Bailey, and was amply rewarded. She was then over eighty-five years of age. She sat reading her Bible when I entered her room, and she arose with a pleasant smile of welcome that brightened her wrinkled face. I had been forewarned that she was a most ardent politician of the Democratic school, and that if I was a political friend of General Taylor, the then Whig candidate for the Presidency of the Republic, I need not expect any information from her, for she could not tolerate a political opponent. So forewarned, I was forearmed; and when her almost first uttered words were, "What are Cass's prospects in New York?" I declared my belief (which was sincere) that he would be elected, and added, with some mental reservation, "At any rate, he *ought* to be elected." This was the key that unlocked the casket of her kindly feeling, and I spent an hour agreeably and profitably with her.

Mrs. Bailey had been made a widow only a very short time before my visit, by the death of her husband, Captain Elijah Bailey, who had held the office of postmaster at Groton for the space of forty years. He was appointed by President Jefferson in 1808. At his death his official mantle was placed upon the shoulders of his venerable widow. He, too, was an ardent politician, but was surpassed in partisan zeal by his wife, who in the embellishment of her room exhibited the intensity of her partisanship. There were lithographed likenesses of Jackson and Van Buren, from whose heads she had received locks of hair, which she showed me. Their portraits were hung in a good light, while those of the Whigs, Clay and Frelinghuysen, were in an obscure place, with their heads downward.

Mrs. Anna Bailey

Mrs. Bailey gave me an interesting account of some of the incidents of that fatal morning at Fort Griswold. The garrison was commanded by Colonel William Ledyard, a native of Groton and a friend of her father. He lived not far from the fort, and the home of Mrs. Bailey was in full sight of it. The invaders were led by the traitor, Benedict Arnold. They landed in two divisions, one under Colonel Eyre, on the east or Groton side of the Thames, and the other, under Arnold, on the New London side. The militia flocked to the fort in such haste that many of them were without arms. Arnold burned New London; Eyre marched against Fort Griswold.[34]

"I saw the American flag that was flying over the southwest bastion shot down," said Mrs. Bailey. "The Hessians made a furious assault on the fort, and a hard fight continued for about three quarters of an hour. Colonel Eyre was mortally wounded, and Major Bromfield (I was told), a wicked New Jersey Tory, took the command. Very soon the assailants broke into the fort, where, as I was told afterward, Bromfield demanded of Colonel Ledyard, 'Who commands this fort?' The colonel politely replied, 'I did, sir, but you do now,' and handed the major his sword. Bromfield immediately ran Colonel Ledyard through with his own sword, and so murdered him. The Hessians and Tories followed the example of their leader, and murdered no less than seventy of the defenseless garrison and badly wounded forty-five others. The savages would not allow the wounded a drop of water. They left during the night by the light of burning New London, which Arnold had set on fire. The next morning I saw Fanny Ledyard, who was visiting the family of the murdered colonel, come crying out of the sally-port, for she had seen the dead body of her uncle. She had gone cautiously into the fort, with two pails of water, not knowing whether the ruffians had left. She was the first to moisten the lips of the poor sufferers."

Mrs. Bailey's late husband, then a youth about seventeen years old, was in the fort just previous to the attack. He and Mr. Williams were ordered to man a gun at a redoubt in advance of the fort. They were directed, in the event of their not being able to resist the enemy successfully, to retreat to the fort. They were compelled to abandon the gun. Williams fled to the fort and was murdered. Young Bailey stopped to spike the gun, and when he reached the fort the gate was closed and barred. He jumped over a fence into a cornfield, where he lay concealed until the battle was over and the massacre was ended, and so he was saved.

"He was courting me, Miss Anna Warner, at that very time, boy as he was," said Mrs. Bailey, as she related the circumstances to me. "I was six months older than he," she said; "just old enough to make him draw the cider after we were married."

Mrs. Bailey had many things to tell me of her experience there during the War of 1812–15—the second war for independence. Commodore Decatur, with the frigates *United States* and *Macedonian*, ran into the Thames up to New London and above in the summer of 1813, and was there blockaded by a British squadron. At one time, when that squadron threatened to bombard New London, the military forces that manned Fort Trumbull, in the harbor, were deficient in flannel for making cannon cartridges. Every family in New London and Groton was visited in search of the needed material, and a considerable quantity was cheerfully sent to the garrison. Mr. Latham, a neighbor of Mrs. Bailey came to her seeking more. She started out and collected all the little petticoats of children that she could find in the village.

"'This is not half enough, Mrs. Bailey,' said Latham to me; 'can't you find more?'

"'You shall have mine too,' I said, as I cut with my scissors the string that held it to my waist and handed it to Latham. It was a heavy new one, which I had spun and woven myself, but I didn't care a groat for that. All I wanted was to have it do duty for my country," and her blue eyes sparkled with the recollection.

When Latham told the story to some of Decatur's men, who were assisting the garrison, they declared it would be a shame to cut up that garment into cartridge patterns; it ought to flutter at the masthead of one of their frigates as an ensign, under which they would fight right gallantly out on the broad ocean. But those frigates had no occasion to raise an ensign or open their ports, for they were kept prisoners in the Thames for the remainder of the war, a period of about twenty months.

Mrs. Bailey gave me an account of the festivities at New London after the President's proclamation of peace, received early in 1815, in which she and her husband participated. On the evening of February 21st a ball was given at the court-house. The town was brilliantly illuminated. Admiral Hotham was the commander of the British squadron blockading the

"I danced two cotillons with him."

Thames. He was brightly esteemed by the citizens, for, like his predecessor, Commodore Hardy, he was a gentleman, and his conduct had been marked by forbearance and courtesy. His flagship was the *Superb*. He determined to join in the festivities on that occasion. Announcing the parole on his ship to be "America," and the countersign "Amity," he and his officers went on shore, mingled freely and cordially with the inhabitants, and danced at the ball with the ladies of New London.

"I was then just fifty years old," said Mrs. Bailey, when telling me the story, "but I was as spry as any of the girls, plump and fair, dressed in a Canton-crêpe gown, low-necked, short-waisted, and short-sleeved. I remember I had a string of gold beads around my neck and white slippers on my feet. The admiral was almost seventy years old, yet he was as frisky as a fox, with a jolly red face and white hair. I danced two cotillons with him. Captain Bailey said I was the prettiest woman at the ball, and he was a good judge. Now, don't laugh at me because of my vanity. I love to remember it because my husband said it," and tears glistened in her eyes.

I have no doubt of the justice of the captain's remark, for at the great age of eighty-five years there were in the face of this remarkable woman remains of former beauty. She was still vivacious, her smile was winning, and her large blue eyes retained much of their former luster. And when, a little later, I asked her permission to make a pencil sketch of her face, she consented with almost coquettish readiness. When I remarked, as I was tracing the outlines, "Captain Bailey was a good judge," she instantly replied:

"I was never ashamed of my face."

Alas! Poor Anna Bailey. On January 10th, 1851, a little more than two years after my visit, her clothes took fire, and she was burned to death at the age of over eighty-seven years. She died the venerable postmistress of Groton.

Chapter XIII
Headquarters at Morristown

In the eastern suburbs of Morristown, N.J., stands the modest mansion used by Washington as the headquarters of the army in the winter of 1779-80. It is as well preserved, with patriotic care, as it was when, in September 1848, I passed a night under its roof in the enjoyment of the hospitality of its proprietor, the Hon. Gabriel Ford, who, a lad of fourteen years, lived there with his widowed mother when the Continental Army was tented and hutted near by during a terrible winter encampment.[35]

The general and his suite occupied the whole house except two rooms on the eastern side of the main passage, in which Mrs. Ford and her family lived. The lower front room on the left of the door was the general's dining-room, and the apartment immediately over it was used as a bedroom when Mrs. Washington was at headquarters. In that room I slept. The same carpet, dark and of a rich pattern, was on the floor that was trodden by Mrs. Washington and her husband nearly seventy years before; also two or three pieces of furniture which their eyes beheld and their hands had touched.

I went to Judge Ford's at an early hour in the evening, and rich were the blessings of most interesting information which I received from the lips of the octogenarian during a sitting of fully three hours.

"Where was the army encamped?" I inquired.

"The main body occupied the southern slope of Kimball's Mountain, the nearest quarters, about two miles from here," he said. "They were near enough to be easily called into sudden action by sentinels placed at points between headquarters and the camp. Several times during the winter night alarms set the soldiers in camp in motion toward headquarters. On such occasions the Life Guard would rush to the house, barricade the doors, and throw up the windows. Five soldiers with their muskets cocked were generally placed at each window, and there they would remain until troops from the camp reached headquarters and the cause of the alarm was ascertained. These occasions were very annoying to Mrs. Washington and my mother, who were obliged to lie in bed, sometimes for hours, with their rooms full of soldiers and the winter air entering the open windows and piercing through their drawn curtains."

"That winter was a very cold one, was it not?" I inquired.

"The hardest winter I ever knew," said the judge. "Early in January the snow was from four to six feet deep. Oh, how the poor soldiers suffered! They were yet in tents, and did not get into huts until February. The roads were almost impassable, and so difficult was it to transport provisions to the army, that sometimes the poor fellows would be six or eight days without meat. New York Harbor froze over so firmly that British troops with cannon passed over the ice-bridge from the city to Staten Island, a distance of nine miles."

"You spoke of the Life Guards rushing into the house. I suppose they were stationed very near?"

"Yes; they occupied about fifty log-huts in the large meadow a few rods from the house. They were about two hundred and fifty strong. A fine set of fellows they were, and thoroughly trained. Before the snow became deep Count Pulaski exercised his legion in that meadow. Some of their feats were wonderful. The dexterity of the count in handling his horse and pistol was amazing. I have seen him, while his horse was at full speed, discharge his pistol, throw it in the air, catch it by the barrel, and then hurl it forward as if at a fleeing

"The dexterity of the count in handling his horse and pistol was amazing."

enemy. Then, without checking his horse, he would slip one foot from the stirrup, and leaning over toward the ground, recover his pistol, and wheel into line with as much precision as if he had been engaged in nothing but the management of his steed."[36]

"Was not General Schuyler at Morristown a while in the spring?" I asked.

"He came from Philadelphia at the close of February, at the request of Washington. Schuyler was in Congress. He was the most trusted counselor and friend of the commander-in-chief, who desired his advice on the arrangement of the campaign the coming season. He came with his wife and his daughter Elizabeth, a charming young woman, took a house, that is yet standing, near the railway station, and there they entertained most hospitably during the few weeks they remained. Soon after their arrival, Colonel Hamilton, Washington's secretary, became acquainted with Schuyler's daughter, was smitten by her personal charms, her vivacity, and her accomplishments, and fell desperately in love with her. He passed almost every evening with her.

"At length," said Judge Ford, "a funny event took place. The colonel seemed to think much of me, and, by permission of the general, would furnish me with the countersign that I might remain at play in the village and return after dark, when the sentinels were set. One evening I was coming home about nine o'clock, and had given the word to the sentinel, when I recognized the voice of Hamilton in reply to the soldier's demand:

"'Who comes there?'

"I stepped aside and waited for the colonel to accompany me to our house.

"Hamilton came up to the point of the sentinel's presented bayonet to give the countersign. He had quite forgotten it. He had spent the evening with Miss Schuyler, and thoughts of her undoubtedly expelled the countersign from his mind. The soldier-lover was embarrassed. The sentinel knew him well, but was stern in the performance of his duty. Hamilton pressed his hand to his forehead and tried to summon the important words from their hiding place, but, like the faithful sentinel, they were immovable. Just then he descried me in the darkness.

"'Ah, Master Ford,' he said in an undertone, 'is that you?' and, stepping aside, he called me to him and whispered:

"'Give me the countersign.'

"I did so, when Hamilton, stepping in front of the soldier, gave it to him. The sentinel, believing that his superior was testing his fidelity, kept his bayonet unmoved.

"'I have given you the countersign, why do you not shoulder your musket?' asked Hamilton.

"'Will that do, colonel?' inquired the sentinel, in reply.

"'It will do for this time; let me pass.'

"The sentinel reluctantly obeyed the illegal command, and we passed on. The lovers were married before the next Christmas. You know the rest. Hamilton was shot by Burr. His widow, I understand, is yet living, over ninety years of age."

"She is," I replied. "She is living with her affectionate daughter, Mrs. Holley, in elegant retirement in Washington City. I expect to see her in a few weeks."

"Did not a distinguished Spanish gentleman die here during that spring?" I inquired.

"Yes," said Judge Ford. "He came with the Chevalier de Luzerne, the French minister, early in April. His name was Miralles—Don Juan De Miralles—a Spanish grandee. They remained at headquarters for some time. A ball was given in honor of the minister at the Morris Tavern, which was attended by General and Mrs. Washington, all his officers,

General and Mrs. Schuyler and their daughter, Governor Livingston and his wife, and many other people of quality. Miralles was prostrated by a heavy cold at the time, and remained in bed at headquarters. He grew worse rapidly, and a day or two before the first of May he died, and was buried in the little cemetery of the Presbyterian Church. During his illness Mrs. Washington administered to his wants with her own hands. A Spanish priest, who was one of his attendants, performed the ceremonies at his funeral. The coffin was borne to the grave on the shoulders of four artillery officers in full uniform, followed by Washington and Luzerne and their respective suites and many citizens. It is said the Spaniard was very rich. I remember looking upon his dead body with wonder, awe, and admiration, as it lay 'in state,' as we say, in the room where we are now sitting, in his richly ornamented open coffin, lined with fine cambric and covered with black velvet. Instead of a shroud, he was in a full-dress suit of scarlet, embroidered with gold lace; a three-cornered gold-laced hat; a cued wig; white silk stockings; large diamond-studded knee and shoe buckles; a prominent diamond ring on his finger, and from a superb gold watch set with diamonds several rich seals were hung. I heard that he left his immense fortune to his three daughters in Spain, amounting to half a million dollars each."

"Was Mrs. Washington at headquarters all winter?" I inquired.

"She came at about the middle of January," said Judge Ford, "when the snow was deepest and the cold most severe and the soldiers were suffering most. Her presence was like sunshine. She had a kind word and act for everybody. The officers accorded homage to her noble character; the soldiers adored her, and yet she was as simple and sweetly dignified in her deportment as a pious matron ought to be. While she could entertain with great cheerfulness, grace, urbanity, and good sense, she was seldom without knitting-work in her hands when receiving and entertaining guests.[37] The suffering of the soldiers touched her generous nature, and she even interested the women of every degree in Morristown in cooperating with her in providing for the sick and suffering in the army."

"And Washington?"

"He was always grave, but never sad; always kind, but never familiar, and he was scrupulously just and thoughtful of duty toward others."

As an illustration of a phase of Washington's private character, Judge Ford related that when the patriot took possession of Mrs. Ford's mansion he made an inventory of all articles which were appropriated to his use during the winter. When he withdrew in the spring he inquired whether everything had been returned to her.

"All but one silver spoon," she said.

He took note of it, and not long afterward she received a spoon from Washington bearing his initials—G.W. It was preserved in the family as a precious memento, and as such it was shown to me the next morning. Washington's tender care for the comfort of Mrs. Ford (who was the widow of Colonel Jacob Ford, commander of the Morris County militia at the time of Washington's flight through New Jersey) was often evinced. On the occasion of the night alarms mentioned, he always went to her room, drew the bed-curtains close, and soothed her with assurances of safety. When her son, a lad of seventeen, was brought home wounded, from Springfield, Washington's first care in the morning was to inquire after the sufferer.

Judge Ford was eighty years of age at the time of my visit. He was well formed and erect in person, about five feet ten inches in stature, with his faculties apparently not at all impaired by age. His memory of dates, names, and events were remarkable. The evening passed with him was, to me, one of the most interesting and profitable of any experience during my pilgrimage to the relics, animate and inanimate, of the period of the old war for independence. Our conversation took a wide range of topics upon one subject—the Revolution and its actors. As I rose to depart, at ten o'clock, the venerable jurist invited me to pass the night under his roof, saying, 'You shall lodge in the very room occupied by Washington and his spouse." I accepted the boon so kindly offered, and soon retired.

From the window of that room, opening southward, I witnessed at near midnight an almost total eclipse of the moon. As from that interesting observatory I watched the progress of the obscuration, and then the gradual enlightenment of the satellite, it appeared to me a most significant cause of the patriots at the time when, from the same window, Washington with anxious eye had doubtless gazed upon the same orb on its silent journey among the stars. It was the gloomiest period of the war. For many months the bright prospects of the patriots were passing deeper and deeper within the penumbra of British power and oppression; and at the beginning of 1780 only a faint curve of light was seen upon the disk of hope; the eclipse was almost total.

Chapter XIV
The Last Surviving Belle of the Revolution

Elizabeth Schuyler, daughter of General Philip Schuyler, was one of the most charming women of her day at almost every period of her long life. Well educated, possessed of many accomplishments, used to the elegances and etiquette of the best social circles of New York, connected by consanguinity with the leading families of the State, richly endowed with a comely person, a sweet and affectionate disposition, and vivacious and witty withal, she was regarded as one of the most attractive belles during a portion of the period of the Revolution. As a young matron, the wife of Colonel Alexander Hamilton, she was an ornament and representative of the best society of the Commonwealth, always lively and gracious, yet dignified; and in the evening shadows of her long life—widow for fifty years—her society was sought by the intellectual and refined.

When, in the spring of 1776, Doctor Franklin, Charles Carroll, and Samuel Chase, a committee of the Continental Congress invested with its delegated powers, went to Canada on a diplomatic mission, they were entertained at Albany by General Schuyler, and by him conveyed to Lake George. Mr. Carroll wrote of the general in his journal:

"He behaved to us with great civility; lives in pretty style; has two daughters (Betsey and Peggy), lively, agreeable, black-eyed gals, who made our stay very pleasant."

These were Elizabeth, afterward Mrs. Hamilton, and Margaret, the future spouse of the Albany patron, Stephen Van Rensselaer.

In the spring of 1780 Miss Schuyler accompanied her parents to the headquarters of the Continental Army at Morristown, N.J., where they tarried several weeks. She attracted much attention. There Colonel Hamilton, Washington's accomplished secretary, enamored by her charms, wooed and won her, and they were married at Albany in December, the same year. From that time she was one of the most beloved and cherished friends of Mrs. Washington until the death of the latter, more than twenty years afterward. Their mutual attachment seemed like that of mother and daughter.

Mrs. Hamilton was deeply affected by the demise of her distinguished friend. Two years later she was compelled a far greater bereavement in the sudden death of her husband, at the age of forty-seven, slain by a pistol ball on the dueling-ground at Weehawken. For fifty years afterward she lived a widow, dying at the home of her only daughter, Mrs. Holley, in Washington City. In a large pocketbook which she carried about her person was found the letter written to her by her husband on the morning of his departure for the fatal field. It was much discolored by her tears. She had carried it in her bosom for half a century.

Mrs. General Alexander Hamilton. Aged 30.

I was in Washington City at the close of 1848, and enjoyed the privilege of passing my first evening there with the venerable widow of General Hamilton. She was then in the ninety second year of her age, and showing few symptoms, in person or mind, of extreme longevity. The sunny cheerfulness of her temper and quiet humor, which had shed their blessed influences around her all through life, still made her deportment genial and attractive. Her memory, faithful to the myriad impressions of a long and eventful experience, was ever ready with its various reminiscences to give a peculiar charm to her conversation

Mrs. General Alexander Hamilton. Aged 94.

upon subjects of the buried past. She was then the last living belle of the Revolution, and possibly the last survivor of the notable women who gave a charm to the Republican court at New York and Philadelphia during Washington's administration.

When I revealed to Mrs. Hamilton the object of my visit, her dark eyes beamed with pleasurable emotion. She seated herself in an easy-chair near me, and we talked without ceasing upon the interesting theme until invited by her daughter to the tea-table, at eight o'clock, where we were joined by a French lady, eight or ten years the junior of Mrs. Hamilton.

Our conversation began abruptly.

"I have lately visited Judge Ford at Morristown," I remarked.

"Judge Ford—Judge Ford," she repeated musingly. "Oh, I remember now! He called on me a few years ago, and brought to my recollection many little events which occurred while I was at Morristown with my father and mother during the war, and which I had forgotten. I remember him as a bright boy, much thought of by Mr. Hamilton, who was then Washington's secretary. He brought to mamma and me from Mrs. Washington an invitation to headquarters soon after our arrival at Morristown."

"Had you ever seen Mrs. Washington before?" I inquired.

"Never. She received us so kindly, kissing us both, for the general and papa were very warm friends. She was then almost fifty years old, but was still handsome. She was quite short—a plump little woman with dark brown eyes, her hair a little frosty, and very plainly dressed for such a grand lady, as I considered her. She wore a plain brown gown of homespun stuff, a large white neckerchief, a neat cap, and her plain gold wedding ring, which she had worn more than twenty years. Her graces and cheerful manner delighted us. She was always my ideal of a true woman. Her thoughts were then much on the poor soldiers who had suffered during that dreadful winter, and she expressed her joy at the approach of milder spring time."

"Were you much at headquarters afterward?" I inquired.

"Only a short time the next winter and an occasional visit," she replied. "We went to New Windsor after we were married, and there a few weeks afterward Mr. Hamilton left the general's military family. I made my home with my parents at Albany, while my husband remained in the army until after the surrender of Cornwallis. I visited Mrs. Washington at headquarters at Newburgh, on her invitation, in the summer of 1782, when I remember she had a beautiful flower garden planted and cultivated by her old stone house standing on the high bank of the river and overlooking a beautiful bay and the lofty highlands beyond. We were taken from Newburgh in a barge to the headquarters of the French army, a little below Peekskill, where we were cordially received by the Viscount De Noailles, a kinsman of Madame Lafayette, who was Mr. Hamilton's warm friend. We remained there several days, and were witness of the excellent discipline of the French troops. There we saw the brave young Irishwoman called 'Captain Molly,' whom I had seen two or three times before. She seemed to be a sort of pet of the French."

"Who was 'Captain Molly,' and for what was she famous?" I asked.

"Why, don't you remember reading of her exploit at the battle of Monmouth? She was the wife of a cannonier—a stout, red-haired, freckled-faced young Irishwoman named Mary. While her husband was managing one of the field-pieces in that action she constantly brought water from a spring near by. A shot from the British killed him at his post, and the officer in command having no one competent fill his place, ordered the piece to be withdrawn. Molly (as she was called) saw her husband fall as she came from the spring, and also heard the order. She dropped her bucket, seized the rammer, and vowed that she would fill the place of her husband at the gun and avenge his death. She performed the duty with great skill, and won the admiration of all who saw her. My husband told me that she was brought in by General Greene the next morning, her dress soiled with blood and dust, and presented to Washington as worthy of reward. The general, admiring her courage, gave her the commission of a sergeant, and on his recommendation her name was placed upon the list of half-pay officers for life. She was living near Fort Montgomery, in the Highlands, at the time of our visit, and came to the camp two or three times while we were there. She was dressed in a sergeant's coat and waistcoat over her petticoat, and a cocked hat. The story of her exploit charmed the French officers, and they made her many presents. She would sometimes pass along the French lines when on parade, and get her hat nearly filled with half-crowns."[38]

"You must have seen and become acquainted with very many of the most distinguished men and women of America, and also eminent foreigners, while your husband was in Washington's Cabinet," I remarked.

"Oh, yes," she replied. "I had little of private life in those days. Mrs. Washington, who, like myself, had a passionate love of home and domestic life, often complained of the 'waste of time' she was compelled to endure. 'They call me the First Lady in the Land, and think I must be extremely happy,' she would say, almost bitterly, at times, and add, 'They might more properly call me the Chief State Prisoner.'

"As I was younger than she I mingled more in the gayeties of the day. I was fond of dancing, and usually attended the public balls that were given. I was at the inauguration ball—the most brilliant of them all—which was given early in May at the Assembly Rooms on Broadway, above Wall Street. It was attended by the President and Vice-President, the Cabinet officers, a majority of the members of Congress, the French and Spanish ministers, and military and civil officers, with their wives and daughters. Mrs. Washington had not yet arrived in New York from Mount Vernon, and did not until three weeks later. On that occasion every woman who attended the ball was presented with a fan, prepared in Paris, with ivory frame, and when opened displayed a likeness of Washington in profile."

"Were you often at balls which Washington attended?" I inquired.

"Frequently."

"Did he usually dance on such occasions?"

"I never saw Washington dance," she replied. "He would always choose a partner and *walk* through the figures correctly, but he never danced. His favorite was the minuet, a slow, graceful dance, suited to his dignity and gravity, and now little known, I believe."

"Mrs. Washington's receptions were very brilliant, were they not?" I asked.

"Brilliant so far as beauty, fashion, and social distinction went," she replied; "otherwise they were very plain and entirely unostentatious."

"Did you usually attend them?" I asked.

"Frequently. I remember a very exciting scene at one of her earlier receptions. Ostrich plumes, waving high over the head, formed a part of the evening headdress of a fashionable belle at that time. Miss McEvers, sister of Mrs. Edward Livingston, who was present, had plumes unusually high. The ceiling of the drawing-room of the President's house, near Franklin Square, was rather low, and Miss McEver's plumes were ignited by the flame of the chandelier. Major Jackson, Washington's aide-de-camp, sprang to the rescue of the young lady, and extinguished the fire by smothering it with his hands."

"You saw many distinguished French people, refugees from the tempest of the revolution in France, did you not?" I inquired.

"Very many. New York became much Frenchified in speech and manners. Mr. Hamilton spoke French fluently, and as he did not sympathize with the revolutionists, who drove the exiles from their homes, he was a favorite with many of the cultivated *émigres*. Among the most distinguished of these was Talleyrand, a strange creature, who stayed in America nearly two years. He was notoriously misshapen, lame in one foot, his manners far from elegant, the tone of his voice was disagreeable, and in dress he was rather slovenly. Mr. Hamilton saw much of him, and while he admired the shrewd diplomat for his great intellectual endowments, he detested his utter lack of principle. He had no conscience. In the summer of 1794 he spent several days with us at the Grange, on Harlem Heights."

"Did you not entertain the young son of Lafayette and his tutor at the Grange a year or two later?" I inquired.

"We did, while they were waiting for Washington to retire from office. They came to this country when the marquis was in an Austrian prison, and his wife and daughter were gladly sharing his fate. Their son, George Washington, was sent to the protection of Lafayette's beloved friend. The President and Mrs. Washington would gladly have received him into their family, but State policy forbade it at that critical time. The lad and his tutor passed a whole summer with us at the Grange. At length he and his pupil went to Philadelphia, lived quietly at private lodgings, and when the retired President and his family left the seat of government for Mount Vernon, the tutor and pupil accompanied them. When the young man and his father were in this country twenty-odd years ago, they very warmly greeted me, for the marquis loved Mr. Hamilton as a brother. Their love was mutual."

I might repeat many more utterances of interesting personal reminiscences of the venerable and venerated matron, but these must suffice. At my request she kindly wrote her name in my notebook. I bade her adieu immediately after tea. Her sweet spirit departed on November 9th, 1854, after a pilgrimage on the earth of ninety-seven years and three months.

Chapter XV
Doctor Franklin's Errand-Boy

"Would you like to be introduced to Doctor Franklin's errand-boy?" asked a friend (John A. McAllister) with whom I was sojourning a few days in Philadelphia, in the year 1861. "He is a most remarkable man," said my friend, "and has been a prominent citizen here for fully sixty years."

"It would be a special privilege," I replied.

We crossed the Schuylkill to West Philadelphia, and made our way to the Pennsylvania Asylum for the Insane. At the entrance gate my friend was warmly greeted by a courteous old gentleman, apparently about sixty-five years of age, who was introduced to me as Colonel Robert Carr, and I was introduced to him as a citizen of New York in quest of reminiscences of events of our long-past history from the lips of survivors of actors in them.

"You bear the whole name, title and all," I said, "of the Irish baronet who was one of the commissioners sent to 'regulate New England,' and to assist in snatching our province from the Dutch two hundred years ago."

"Of the same family stock, probably, for I was born in Ireland," he replied. "Come in, gentlemen, and be seated. It is an early hour, and we shall have few interruptions."

He led the way to a small, nearly furnished room, and there we spent about two hours very profitably with the venerable gatekeeper of the asylum and the errand-boy of Doctor Franklin, who was then over eighty-three years of age, and whose career had been checkered by many vicissitudes. He was a stout-built, vigorous man, possessed of sound health and remarkable buoyancy of spirits. He assured me that he had not been sick in over sixty years.

"You say you were born in Ireland. My friend tells me that your life has been an eventful one," I remarked.

"Somewhat," he said. "But it is now well-nigh over," he continued. "I try to forget the miseries, which are now few, and to remember the mercies, which are many."

At my request he gave a brief sketch of his life's history. He was brought to Philadelphia from Ireland by his parents when he was six years of age. His father was a school teacher, and lived next door to Doctor Franklin. In due time young Carr learned the art of printing with Mr. Bache, Franklin's grandson, and soon rose to the head of his profession in Philadelphia. In 1804, when he was only twenty-six years old, he was awarded the first prize of a society, for the best specimens of printing, on exhibition. He was employed to print Wilson's *Ornithology* from the manuscript; also a reprint of *Rees's Cyclopoedia*. As a young member of the famous Philadelphia military corps known as the "McPherson Blues," he was one

of the firing squad on the occasion of the celebration of Washington's funeral, observed by Congress, then in session at Philadelphia. Five of his associates were living in that city at the time of my visit—namely, Samuel Breck, age ninety; S. Palmer, age eighty-one; S.F. Smith, aged eighty-one; Charles N. Banker, aged eighty-five; Quinton Campbell, aged eighty-five. I saw three of the five veterans at that time.

In 1812 Mr. Carr was commissioned major of a Pennsylvania regiment of infantry, and rose to lieutenant-colonel the following year. Serving faithfully all through the War of 1812–15, Colonel Carr was honorably discharged at its close, and for many years he was the sole survivor of the field officers of the army of 1812 in Pennsylvania, New Jersey, and Delaware. He married a daughter of William Bartram, the proprietor of the famous Botanic Garden, near Philadelphia,[39] and in right of his wife, after her father's death, he carried it on from 1808 until 1850, a period of more than forty years. He served the State as adjutant-general a few years, and was for a long time an alderman and justice of the peace in Philadelphia. In his days of prosperity he was an active promoter of public enterprises. Deprived of his property by the vicissitudes of fortune in his old age, he accepted the position of gatekeeper at the institution where we found him.

"Our friend tells me," I remarked, "that you were an errand-boy for Doctor Franklin for a while."

"Oh, yes," he replied; "I served him as such for the space of nearly two years. We lived next door to Doctor Franklin, in Market Street, and he seemed to think much of my father, who was frequently in his house, by invitation. I sometimes went there with my father, and Franklin treated me very kindly, having always a pleasant word for me. I was about ten years old when he asked my father to allow me to do errands for him. Young as I was, he sent me everywhere, and I was very proud. He sent me to the butcher, the grocer, the printers, the book-stores, the doctor, and to different gentlemen in the city. He was sick most of the time while I was with him, often suffering a great deal from his malady, and yet he continued to write a great deal. I think he wrote two or three pamphlets during the last year of his life. I carried his manuscripts to the printers, and also the proof-sheets. His grandson, Benjamin Franklin Bache, then just out of college, who was much with his grandfather, assisted him in reading the proof sheets. The young man started a newspaper in the fall after Franklin died, and it was in his establishment that I learned the trade of a printer."

"Were you living with Franklin at the time of his death?" I inquired.

"Yes; for three months before he died I was in his room a great deal, to do errands for the doctor, for his attendant (Mrs. Hewson), and for the family. For two or three weeks, I remember, Doctor Jones[40] came several times every day, and sometimes brought Doctor Rush with him."

"Do you distinctly remember the personal appearance of Franklin?" I inquired.

"Perfectly," he answered. "It made a strong impression on my young mind. When I first began to do errands for him he was quite well—went out frequently and received much company. He was then a strong-built man, over eighty years of age, about five feet nine inches in stature, and inclined to corpulency. His complexion was fair, though he was an old man; his eyes were gray and very bright when he was engaged in conversation; his hair was thin and long, but not very gray; his mouth was not large, and had a decidedly sweet expression. Franklin was polite and kind to everybody, whether he was a servant or a senator, for he was always a gentleman. I remember when Washington called to see him, while on his way to New York to be inaugurated President of the United States. They embraced like brothers. Franklin had been suffering much pain that morning, but was relieved at the time of the President's call, when his manner was cheerful, almost playful at times, for he was rejoiced to see his friend. They never met again on the earth."

"You say you learned the printer's trade in the establishment of Mr. Bache, Franklin's grandson," I remarked.

"Yes; I was his apprentice from 1792 to 1797. After I had been with him a year, finding me rather expert in detecting errors in proof sheets, I was frequently employed as assistant proof reader and in carrying the corrected sheets to the writers for his paper, the *Advertiser*. When the Government was removed to Philadelphia from New York, Washington was very friendly to Mr. Bache, because he was a near kinsman of Franklin, and occasionally

"I carried his manuscripts to the printers, and also the proof-sheets."

wrote something on public matters for the *Advertiser*. He also had official papers printed at our office. I carried corrected proof sheets to President Washington, and sometimes assisted him in the reading and making proper printers' marks for corrections, which he did not always understand."

"So you were once an errand-boy for Doctor Franklin and Washington's assistant proof reader," I remarked.

"It is even so, and I am proud of the service," said the veteran, with a bright smile of satisfaction. "But Washington's friendship for Bache soon cooled," he continued. "Jefferson gained the control of Bache and his newspaper, politically, after Freneau left the city. He was a violent political enemy of Hamilton, you know, and many articles were published in Bache's paper abusing the Secretary of the Treasury and other leaders of the Federal Party, not even sparing the President. The name of the *Advertiser* was changed to that of *Aurora*. In it were published most scandalous attacks upon Washington's administration. I distinctly remember the great excitement in Philadelphia caused by an outrageous article in the *Aurora* against Washington, a day or two after he retired from the Presidency, in the spring of 1797.[41] I well remember that the butchers of Spring Garden, who had been soldiers under Washington, were so incensed that they marched in a body to attack the *Aurora* office. They threw its types into the street and nearly destroyed the inside of the rooms."

"Political excitement ran high at that time, did it not?" I asked.

"Never more violent since," he replied. "Why, for a while it separated families and religious denominations in social intercourse. The pulpits became political rostrums. I remember that in May, 1797, on a day of fasting and prayer, the ministers, by their violent denunciations from the pulpit of 'Jacobins,' secret societies, and philosophers, almost created a riot. The excitable population of Philadelphia were specially incited to violence against the Republicans, or Democrats, who were thus denounced. Fearing violence, Bache, with armed friends, so protected the *Aurora* office that no damage was done. Mr. Bache was personally assaulted on the street, but was not much injured; but the same year he fell a victim to the terrible scourge of yellow-fever, which smote the city fearfully."

"You mentioned Mr. Freneau, the poet of the Revolution. Did you know him personally?" I inquired.

"Very well, though not intimately," he answered, "for he left Philadelphia while I was yet an apprentice sixteen or seventeen years old. He was small in stature, slightly built, but robust in appearance, having followed the sea for many years. He was of Huguenot descent, and about forty years old when I first saw him. His eyes were dark and brilliant; his hair was a rich dark brown; his smile was exceedingly captivating; his voice was sweet; his whole face beamed with intelligence, and his deportment indicated a true gentleman. Mr. Jefferson first employed him as a translating clerk of the State Department, but he was soon engaged in editing a newspaper which was the organ of the Republican Party. It was more violent in its attacks upon Hamilton and Washington's public policy than Bache's paper was afterward. Long years subsequently Freneau acknowledged that many of the most violent articles were written by Jefferson himself. But Jefferson must not be blamed," said Colonel Carr, "for at that time he was really a monomaniac on the subject of miscalled French 'democracy.' He had lately come from France, and was thoroughly imbued with the spirit of the radical French revolutionists. Freneau, you know, celebrated in stirring verse the American victories during the War of 1812-15. Poor Freneau! He perished in a cold storm near Freehold, N.J., in December 1832, when in the eightieth year of his age."

"Did you know, personally, Charles Thomson, the permanent Secretary of the Continental Congress?" I inquired.

"I knew him quite intimately for several years," replied Colonel Carr. "I first became partially acquainted with him about the year 1800. He was then busy in making his translation of the Septuagint, or Old Testament Scriptures, from the original Greek, into English. He also translated the New Testament. I had the reputation then of being the most careful proof reader in Philadelphia, and when Mr. Thomson began to have his great work put in type, he employed me to read the last revised proofs. The whole Bible translated by Mr. Thomson was published by Jane Aitkin, daughter of Robert Aitkin, the printer and publisher of the Bible, at the suggestion or on the recommendation of Congress. Thomson's translation was published in four volumes, in 1808, at about the time when I left printing and took charge of the Botanic Garden."

"What was the personal appearance of Mr. Thomson?" I inquired.

"He was past seventy years of age when I first became acquainted with him. He was rather tall, quite spare in flesh; his face was very thin and much furrowed; his blue eyes were truly sparkling, and his straight white hair hung in graceful curls at the end below his ears. His whole appearance was venerable; yet his form was erect, his step elastic, and his voice was strong, clear, and musical. He lived, as you know, until 1824, when he was in the ninety-fifth year of his age."

I gathered much more from the lips of the venerable printer and soldier during our memorable interview that was exceedingly interesting. He was about to communicate some of his reminiscences of the War of 1812-15 when he was called away by the arrival of visitors at the gate, and we bade him farewell. He afterward committed to writing for me some of his reminiscences of the second war for independence.

Colonel Carr remained very active almost to the last. A month before my visit he went among the Union camps, near Arlington Heights, Va., where he traveled seventeen miles one day, and attended a theatre at Washington City that evening. "I could have danced a cotillon after that," he said. In 1863 he participated in the centennial celebration of the birth of William Bradford, the first printer in Pennsylvania and New York, held by the New York Historical Society; and on February 22d, 1864, when he was past eighty-six years of age, he read Washington's Farewell Address before the veterans of the War of 1812 at Philadelphia. He died on April 15th, 1866.

Chapter XVI
Washington's Last Surviving Bondwoman

On March 4th, 1853, I stood for nearly two hours in the open area at the eastern front of the Capitol at Washington, with thousands of my fellow citizens, pelted with sharp sleet driven by a keen northeast wind, to witness the inauguration of the fourteenth President of the United States. I had no "friends at court" to secure shelter for me under the superb and spacious portico of the Capitol, where the great officers of State, of the judiciary, of the army and of the navy, and foreign ministers were congregated.

For the purpose of this quadrennial coronation of a Chief Magistrate of the Republic, a rude platform of rough boards had been erected over the entrance steps of the Capitol. The whole ceremony was severely simple. The recipient of the exalted dignity about to be conferred was clad in a plain suit of black cloth. A small mahogany table covered with a red cloth, of the value of five dollars, and bearing a Bible, a brown stone pitcher full of cold water, and a ten-penny cut-glass tumbler, constituted the entire paraphernalia. With his head bared to the pelting storm, and his right hand lifted toward Heaven before the Chief Justice of the United States, the new President pledged his fidelity to the Constitution, by affirmation. Then turning to the multitude present, a fraction of the whole power which he represented, he enunciated the fundamental principles which should govern his actions. The multitude shouted prolonged plaudits. The President bowed and retired, and that was the end of the matter.

How little—how exceedingly insignificant to the eye of the true philosopher and hopeful apostle of freedom—would any ruler by the grace of bayonets and gunpowder have appeared upon that rough platform of New Hampshire pine, with all his gaudy trappings and pomp of manner, by the side of Franklin Pierce, the chosen servant of State of a mighty people, who stood there in all the dignity of a true sovereign, but undistinguished in form and bearing from the humble citizen by ribbon or cross, by star or garter, by scepter or crown!

Among those who sat under the shelter of the grand portice of the Capitol on that occasion was George Washington Parke Custis, the adopted son of the "Father of his Country," the first President of the nation, chosen by a popular vote, and the only survivor of the executors of the great Patriot's Will. He was present when his foster-father took the oath of office administered by Chancellor Livingston, in the street gallery of the old City Hall at New York, sixty-four years before. He had witnessed the inauguration of every President from Washington to Pierce. Unmindful of the wind and sleet, he had crossed the Potomac from Arlington House in an open boat, to assist at the august ceremonial. I accepted his cordial invitation to spend a few days at Arlington House, where I had been a guest a few times. I crossed the ferry at Georgetown on the first bright morning thereafter, and found Mr. Custis in his studio giving some touches to his picture of "The Surrender of Yorktown."

The mansion (yet standing) occupies a commanding site, over three hundred feet above tidewater, overlooking the cities of Washington and Georgetown, with the broad Potomac flowing between. The building is of brick, and presents a front, including the two wings, of one hundred and forty feet. The grand portico, having eight massive Doric columns, occupies an area of sixty feet front and twenty-five feet in depth. A park of two hundred acres, dotted with groves of oak and chestnut trees, and cultivated on the riverbank, sloped eastward from the front; and behind the mansion was an old forest abounding with patriarchal trees centuries old, and covering the hills and dales of over eight hundred acres.

A portion of this forest has since disappeared, and the soil is occupied by the remains of thousands of Union soldiers who perished in the great Civil War of 1861–65. On the verge of this cemetery stands a chaste marble monument erected to the memory of Mr. Custis. Near the northern end of the mansion stood a venerable weeping willow, the offspring of a twig plucked by a young British officer from the famous willow planted by Pope at Twickenham, and presented to the father of Mr. Custis by that officer, at Cambridge in 1775. That twig, which the elder Custis planted at Abingdon (his estate nearer Mount Vernon), became the progenitor of all the weeping willows in the United States.

Arlington House was plethoric with precious mementos of the Washington and Custis families, consisting of some rare works of art, plate, china, furniture, ornaments, and a large quantity of valuable manuscripts. On the walls hung a Kit-Kat portrait, life size, of Colonel Daniel Parke, the ancestor of Mr. Custis, who carried to Queen Anne the news of Marlborough's victory at Blenheim. It was painted by Sir Godfrey Kneller. Near it hung a picture of an old Reformer, painted by Van Dyke. There also were the three-quarter length portraits of Daniel Parke and Martha Custis, by Woolaston. There were other portraits of the Washington and Custis families. One of these was the portrait of Washington in the costume of a Virginia colonel at the age of forty years, painted by Charles Willson Peale. Near this picture, suspended from the ceiling was a lantern, formerly the property of Lawrence Washington, which hung in the great passage at Mount Vernon fully eighty years. There was also the black-walnut sideboard used in the dining-room at Mount Vernon, of elegant workmanship; Washington's massive silver tea-services, made at New York in 1789 of the old family plate; also pieces of the Sèvres porcelain dinner and tea sets, called the "Cincinnati china," because they were presented to General and Madam Washington by French officers, and which bore pictures of the Order of the Society of the Cincinnati, delicately painted. With this china came, as a present to Washington, from the same officers, an elegant jeweled Order, which he wore as President of the General Society of the Cincinnati. It has been worn by successive presidents of the society ever since.

In all the rooms at Arlington House were pieces of furniture and many other objects which were once at Mount Vernon. In an upper chamber was the bed on which Washington died, held too sacred for use; and in another room was the large war tent, or *marquee*, of the general which was used at Yorktown. It was encased in two large leathern pouches.

On my first visit at Arlington House, in 1848, I saw a living relic of the Washington family more interesting than all the rest. Mrs. Custis, *née* Fitzhugh, a charming woman,

Christlike in character and disposition, and saint-like in her works of benevolence and her perennial goodness, then presided over the household at Arlington. She was like a mother and a guardian angel in her care for the physical and spiritual comfort of their slaves, and was a blessing to the poor far and near. She was a most gentle creature—slight in frame, sweet in the expression of her fair face; her voice was soft and musical, and she retained much of her early personal beauty. Her piety was fervid but unostentatious, and her presence was like sunlight in a room. She conducted family worship morning and evening, while her husband, standing, invoked a blessing at every meal.

On the morning after my arrival at Arlington House, in 1848, Mrs. Custis, when ready to read the Scriptures, stepped to a room near by and led out a very aged colored woman, not of quite pure African blood, who was much afflicted with rheumatism. Mrs. Custis helped her to kneel by her side during prayer, and then assisted her to rise and return to her room. After the door was closed I made inquiries concerning the old woman.

"She is the last survivor of the bondservants of the Washington family at Mount Vernon," Mrs. Custis remarked. "I do not know her age precisely, but I think she must be nearly ninety years old. She remembers the hunting-parties at Mount Vernon before the Revolution. She was such a good caretaker of children that she became the nurse of Mr. Custis and his sisters in their infancy. On the death of Mrs. Washington she remained at Mount Vernon in the family of Judge Washington, who inherited the estate, until we were married, in 1804, when at her earnest request she came to live with us, and became the nurse of our four daughters, only one of whom (Mary, the wife of Colonel Lee) grew to womanhood. Eleanor, who now lives with me, was Mary's nurse or care-taker from her fourth to her twelfth year. Westford, Judge Washington's servant, is her nephew, and is yet at Mount Vernon.[42] They much resemble each other."

"Is she intelligent, and is her memory trustworthy?" I inquired.

"She is remarkably intelligent, and her memory of events in her earlier years seems perfectly clear."

"Would it be agreeable to you to allow me to have some conversation with her?" I inquired.

"Perfectly so," responded Mrs. Curtis. "She is a little deaf, but you can easily make her understand you."

Mrs. Curtis went to her room, and soon returning, said, "You can see her an hour after breakfast."

I found the aged woman sitting in an armchair knitting stockings, her room in perfect order. Seated near her it was easy to converse. Her dialect was that of the colored people in general, which I shall not attempt to imitate in this record. I made many inquiries of her touching the daily life of her master and mistress, and received satisfactory answers. I asked her if she remembered the young Martha Custis—the "dark lady"—who died before she was seventeen years of age.

"In course I do," she answered. "I was a smart gal, almost as old as she was. Oh, she was so purty and so good! It seemed as if the Lord wanted her, sure, and thought she was too good to stay in this wicked world. Her dying made master and mistress almost sick and very sorry for a long time, they loved her so; and poor Master Jack, her brother, took it so hard we thought he'd go crazy. But somehow he soon got over it. I 'spects it was 'cause he got in love with Miss Nelly Calvert, and married her soon afterward. She was so purty, too! They lived at Abingdon, not far from Mount Vernon, most of the time after the war was begun;

"I was building a fire in mistress' room, one frosty morning, just at daylight."

and I lived with them from the time when their first baby was born until Master Jack joined master to go and fight Cornwallis. Then he left young mistress and her four children at Mount Vernon."

"Master Jack, as you call him, never came back alive," I said.

"Oh, he didn't!" she exclaimed. "It was drefful, drefful! He was so good, and everybody loved him so. Oh, it was so drefful! I was building a fire in mistress' room, one frosty morning, just at daylight," she continued, "when there was a loud knock at the west door. I ran and opened it, and there stood a soldier holding the bridle of his very sweaty horse, who handed me a letter, and said, 'Tell your mistress that Cornwallis is whipped and a prisoner.'

I ran and told her. She was very happy, and thanked the good Lord. Then she sent me to tell the stable-boy to take care of the soldier's horse, and tell the soldier to stay to breakfast. When I came back mistress was just dressed. She went to Master Jack's room to tell the good news to his wife. When she came back she opened the letter. It was from master, and told her that Master Jack was very sick at the house of his uncle, Colonel Bassett, at Eltham, in Kent, and might not get well. Oh, how troubled the poor women were! The coachmen was ordered to make the big carriage and best horses ready as quick as possible; and as soon as we had breakfasted, the two women, the two younger children, and me to take care of them, started for Eltham. We traveled all day and a greater part of the night as fast as we could, stopping only to feed the horses. We found Master Jack dying with the camp-fever, so Doctor Craik told us.

"Master came at daybreak. He rode all night from Yorktown. A few minutes after he came Master Jack died. Then master and mistress were alone in a room for a while, and young mistress and I and the children were in another room. By and by master and mistress came in. He took young mistress' hand and said many kind words to comfort her. She was crying and sobbing as if her heart would break. Mistress told me afterward that he said to the poor mother that he would take the two children that were there, Nelly and Georgie, and bring them up as his own. And he did. Nelly, who was then nearly three years old, and Georgie, who was a baby, lived at Mount Vernon until master himself died. Georgie—Mr. Custis—lived there until mistress died, more than two years afterward."

"Were you in the room when your master died?" I asked.

"I was there a few minutes before he died. I came up to the room—it was an upper chamber—with something. I remember seeing Christopher (who had taken the place of old Billy as master's body-servant) and his wife Charlotte and Molly the seamstress standing at one end of the room, looking much troubled. A few minutes afterward Molly came down and told me master was dead."

"And you were with your mistress when she died?"

"Oh, yes," she answered; "all the time, for I was to her what Christopher was to master. She died of fever. That morning I took into her room a large bunch of flowers from the fields, for it was a warm day in May. I remember how sweetly she smiled. The fever had left her, and she was very pale, and so weak that she could hardly speak in a whisper. Oh, she was so good! She appeared to me like an angel lying there. At dusk that night she was an angel, for she had gone to heaven."

A few weeks after one of my visits at Arlington House, in the spring of 1853, Mrs. Custis departed from earth, and in the fall of 1857 her husband followed her. The spirit of the last relic of the bondservants of the Beloved Patriot departed in the summer of 1855.

Chapter XVII
Twin Sisters of Croton

On a pleasant day in early March 1860, I crossed the Hudson River in a small boat with an expert oarsman, from the western shore of Tappan Bay to the mouth of the Croton River. I was then on the quest for materials for my *Hudson from the Wilderness to the Sea*, first published in the London *Art Journal*. We passed little squadrons (formerly Teller's) Point, visiting the pretty Italian villa and the vineyards of Doctor Underhill, where hundreds of tons of luscious grapes were raised every year. We then rowed up Croton Bay and passed under the drawbridge of the Hudson River Railway into the mouth of the Croton River. We found the current of the stream very rapid, for the tide in the Hudson was ebbing.

When nearly abreast the Van Cortlandt Manor-house, the oarsman found it impossible to stem the current any longer, and as the water was too shallow to bear the boat to the right bank, as I desired, I was landed on the rugged left bank. I clambered up the acclivity along the margin of a little brook, cheered by the notes of (to me) the first bluebird of the season, perched on a spray overhead. Following the post-road that skirted the elevated shore of the stream, I reached the rickety "high bridge"—the famous "Croton Bridge" of Revolutionary times—at near sunset. It was a picturesque structure, spanning a rocky gorge, through which the Croton River was running rapidly. Near the bridge I obtained a charming view of the mouth of the Croton, with Dover Kill Island near, the broad Tappan Bay, and the blue hills in the distance beyond.

After making a sketch of the old bridge I strolled down the road on the high right bank of the Croton, as it sloped toward the Hudson, and reached the Van Cortlandt Manor-house at twilight. At its entrance gate I met Colonel Pierce Van Cortlandt, the proprietor of the estate, and accepted his cordial invitation to pass the night under his roof. I was kindly welcomed by Mrs. Van Cortlandt, a daughter of the eminent Professor T. Romeyn Beck, of Albany. The house, yet preserved in its ancient aspect, is near the shore of what was once the upper part of the beautiful Croton Bay, in which vessels of considerable size often anchored, and which was also the resort of vast flocks of wild ducks and shoals of shad. Early in 1841 heavy rains and melting snows caused the sweeping away of the great Croton Dam, then recently built, and an immense volume of water released rushed riverward, carrying with it loosened earth sufficient to half fill Croton Bay and convert much of it into a shallow stream.

The Van Cortlandt Manor-house was erected at the beginning of the last century by John Van Cortlandt, son of Stephen Van Cortlandt, the first proprietor of the great domain, whose father, Oloff Stevens Van Cortlandt, was a lineal descendant of the Dukes of Courland, in Russia. His ancestors, when deprived of their duchy, emigrated to Holland, whence Oloff came to New Netherland in 1630, in the service of the Dutch West India Company. The family name was Stevens or Stevenssen, that of Van Cortlandt being only titular. The family became allied by marriage, in time, with the Van Rensselaers, the Schuylers, the Bayards, the De Peysters, the Livingstons, and other leading families in the province and State.

The manor-house was built of heavy stone, and the thick walls of the basement story were pierced with loopholes for the use of musketry, in defense. These still remain. The mansion commands, from its broad piazza in front, an extensive view to the southwest of Tappan Bay and the rugged hills beyond. It is sheltered on the north by a high hill covered with sturdy forest trees.

At the time of my visit there was a broad lawn at the front, and a path led through the old garden to the ancient ferry-house, a building occupied during the Revolution as a guard-house. The Baron De Kalb was stationed there in 1778, and in the winter of 1782 a detachment of New York levies, having just returned there from a scout to Morrisania, were surprised at a barn near the ferry-house by some of the enemy's cavalry. One of the "Continentals" was killed; the remainder escaped on the ice.

The broad entrance hall of the mansion was adorned by the horns of stately stags, killed on the manor when wild deer roamed over the domain. The rooms were enriched with many family portraits, ancient and modern, and other works of art; and the library displayed many precious mementoes of the colonial and Revolutionary period, sufficient to hold the attention of the curious antiquary for days.

On the morning after my arrival at the manor house Mrs. Van Cortlandt invited me to visit aged twin sisters living at the village of Croton, about two miles up the river. She kindly accompanied me to introduce me to the nonagenarians—they were over ninety years of age. On the way we drove into the beautifully situated cemetery of the Van Cortlandt family, on the summit of a hill west of the mansion. It commanded an extensive view of the Hudson southward, with the entire range of the Palisades from Piermont to Hoboken.

At a little west of the cemetery, at the neck which connects Croton Point with the mainland, was pointed out the site of the old fort or castle of *Kitch-a-wan* (the original name of the Croton River). It is said to have been the oldest Indian fort south of the Highlands. It was built by the Sachem Croton, and there he gathered his parties for hunting or for war. At a little east of the site of the fort we came to *Kitch-a-wan* burying-ground, in a beautiful nook at the entrance to Haunted Hollow, concerning which old superstitions supplied many weird stories of early times. The people believed that they saw in the groves and glens the forms of the departed red-men, whom they called the Walking Sachems of Teller's Point.

Only one of the twin sisters could be seen—Mrs. Miriam Williams—the other, Mrs. Eunice McCord, being too feeble in mind and body to receive visitors. Their maiden name was Teller, and they had long been widows. They were descendents of Andrew Teller, who in 1671 married a daughter of Oloff Stevensson Van Cortlandt and a sister of the first proprietor of the Van Cortlandt Manor. Teller's Point received its name from a descendent of his who occupied it.

The memory of Mrs. Williams seemed to be but very little impaired by age, her recollections of her childhood and early womanhood being very vivid. She well remembered incidents connected with the encampment of the American army at Verplanck's Point, in the fall of 1782. She and her sister were then twelve years of age. She remembered seeing

Miriam Williams and Eunice McCord

Washington ride up to the gate in front of their house one day, with only a single attendant, dismount, and ask her father, who was standing near, for some food, as he had been detained on business below. The twins were standing at the door as the general entered the house, and placing his hands on their heads, he said:

"You look as much alike as two eggs; may you have long life."

"The wish of the great man has been granted," said Mrs. Williams, "for we *have* lived long. We were ninety years old last August. We had very little in the house at that time wherewith to entertain such a guest. My mother could set upon the little table only some cold ham, fresh rye bread, sweet butter, a bit of cheese, and some cold water. We children were peeping through the open door into the room, and I remember as well as if it happened yesterday seeing General Washington, before sitting down to partake of the simple meal, place one hand on the table and closing his eyes ask a blessing. Father, meanwhile, stood with his head uncovered in the farther part of the room. And here," said Mrs. Williams, "is the very table at which General Washington stood and asked a blessing," pointing to a small oval table standing near her.

"You seem to have much bodily strength and good health," I remarked, "for a woman so old."

"Yes," she answered; "sister and I have never had any dangerous sickness. We were married when we were quite young; have always lived prudent and generally happy lives;

always had plenty of sleep, and were no gadabouts, as most women are nowadays. Why, you'll hardly believe me when I tell you that neither of us was ever more than five or six miles from where we were born. The Tellers are a strong-bodied and long-lived people."

The story related to me a few hours later was a confirmation of the assurance that the Tellers possessed great bodily vigor.

"Do you remember the French army encamping near here the same fall when you saw General Washington?" I inquired.

"Oh, yes," she said. "They came from the south. They crossed the river at King's Ferry, and all marched by our house. They encamped at Crompond, below here. I remember how afraid and yet delighted sister and I were as we watched them from our window as they passed by. We never saw so many soldiers, nor such glittering uniforms as some of the officers wore, and we never heard such drums beat. We were bewildered with the show, and dreamed of it many nights afterward."

I said farewell to the venerable woman on whose head the hand of Washington had been laid and to whom kind words had been uttered by his lips. At her carriage, in front of Mrs. Williams's house, I parted company with Mrs. Van Cortlandt, and soon afterward rode to the house of a friend about two miles farther north. With a neighbor of his we climbed to the top of Prickly Pear Hill, the summit of which, five hundred feet above the river, was quite thickly strewn in some places with a species of cactus bearing the name of "prickly pear," from which the eminence derived its title.

From the elevation we obtained a most extensive view of the lower Hudson and its shores and a cluster of localities of the most stirring events of the old war for independence. That pinnacle Washington made his chief point of observation while the American army was encamped near, in the fall of 1782. There Washington and his officers, and Rochambeau and his French officers, had viewed the scenery together with profound admiration. At one sweep of the vision might be seen the lofty crags of the Highlands and the Fishkill Mountains stretching eastward, with all the intervening country adjacent, to Peekskill, Verplanck's Point, and Stony Point, the theatres of important military events during the War of the Revolution, then drawing to a close. Before them was Haverstraw, near which Arnold and André complotted; Teller's Point, off which the *Vulture* lay when André went to meet Arnold, and from which she received a cannonading that drove her down the river; King's Ferry, where the American armies crossed and recrossed the Hudson, and from which André made his way to the eastern shore; Tarrytown, where he was captured, and the Long Wharf at Piermont, near Tappan, where he was executed. All these, with the villages on the eastern bank of the Hudson, from Cruger's to York Island, might be seen.

As we were looking at Teller's Point, projecting far toward the western shore of the Hudson, I remarked that I had a most interesting interview at Croton that morning with a member of the Teller family, a woman ninety years of age, and possessed of exceedingly great physical vigor.

"One of the twin sisters?" said one of the gentlemen. "I never knew a Teller who was not possessed of an abundance of bone and sinew. Have you ever heard the story of a Fishkill bully who encountered a young daughter of a Teller living in this neighborhood?"

"I have not."

"Oh, you must hear it. That Teller had two buxom daughters, a little more than twenty years of age. It is said that either of them could lift a barrel of cider. Their father was noted for great strength, and also for wrestling and pugilistic skill. One day, at the close of the

Revolution, a large, rough-looking man came to the door of Teller's house—an old-fashioned double door—and leaning on the under one, the upper one being open, asked one of the daughters within, in a rude manner:

"'Is Bill Taller home?'

"'My father is not at home,' answered the girl. 'What do you want of him? I attend to his business when he is away.'

"'You can't 'tend to 't this time, anyhow. Nobody but Bill Taller himself can,' said the gruff man.

"'Come in and tell me what your business is,' said the girl, as she opened the door.

"The man went in, and she closed it after him, leaving the upper door still open.

"'Now tell me,' said the daughter, 'what your business is, and see if I can't attend to it.'

"'No, you can't, I tell ye,' growled the man. 'I'm Pete Tuttle, of Fishkill, the boss rastler up there. Maybe you've hearn on me. They tell me Bill Taller is the boss rastler down here, and I'm come down to find out who's the best rastler.'

"'Oh, if that's all the business you have,' said the spirited girl, 'I can attend to it at once,' and seizing the man by his coat-collar and the seat of his breeches, she threw him over the door into the grass before it.

"The man picked himself up, and looking in astonishment a few moments at the girl, who was standing in the door with arms akimbo and smiling placidly, he sneaked off without uttering a word.

"'Any more business to be attended to?' asked the girl in a provokingly pleasant voice. The man was too crestfallen to tarry a moment. He joined some companions at the river, who were waiting for him to return with Teller and give them the excitement of a tussle.

"'Didn't you see Teller?' asked one of the company.

"'Naw, I didn't,' said the fellow in a tone of supreme disgust; 'I see one of old Taller's gals, and that's all I want to know.'"

Chapter XVIII
A Surgeon of the Continental Army

I was in New Haven, Conn., late in September 1848, and enjoyed the privilege of a long and interesting interview with Doctor Eneas Munson, who was associated with Doctor James Thacher as a surgeon's mate in the Continental Army. I was introduced to him in his study, and when I told him that I was on a pilgrimage to the abodes of living men and women and the notable places and things connected with the old war for independence, he gave me a cordial welcome and was readily communicative.

I called at Doctor Munson's residence early in the afternoon. He had just risen from his accustomed after dinner repose of an hour or less. "Not always sleeping," he said, "but lying in a healthful, half-conscious revery, which is often more restful than a sound slumber." He seemed as vigorous as a man of sixty, though in the eighty-sixth year of his age. In figure he was rather portly, with a full, fair, and unwrinkled face, a clear eye, a mouth of sweet expression—benevolence beaming in his whole countenance—and a voice strong and kindly. He had inherited from his father (who, at the time of his death, at the age of ninety-two years, had been a practicing physician for seventy years[43]) not only a profession, but uncommon mental and physical vigor. He, too, had practiced the healing art for almost as many years.

"You were a surgeon in the Continental Army, were you not?" I inquired.

"In the spring of 1780 I became an assistant of Doctor James Thacher, then a young surgeon of twenty-six, who had joined the army as such in 1775. I was only eighteen years old. I joined Doctor Thacher at Morristown in April. The winter had been a most severe one. Snow-storms had followed each other in quick succession until, at the middle of January, snow lay on the wooded hills of East Jersey almost six feet deep. The soldiers, first in tents and then in huts, lay at night on beds of straw with only one blanket. They were sometimes nearly famished, being put on short rations—sometimes half or even quarter rations—and often without meat for several days. I remember with pleasure how kindly I was received by the learned director of the General Hospital, Doctor Shippen, and how pleased I was one day on being directed by him to take a little package of medicine to headquarters for a sick Spanish gentleman who was there, having come as a visitor with Luzerne, the French minister. I was told to give the medicine to no one excepting Mrs. Washington, who attended to the sick man's wants continually. That was the first time I ever saw Lady Washington, as the soldiers called her. The Spanish gentleman died, lay in state, and had a grand funeral, which Washington and all his officers attended."[44]

"Was not the army inoculated with the small-pox at Morristown?" I inquired.

"Not then," he answered. "Many of the soldiers had been inoculated there three years before. There was a general inoculation of the troops stationed in the Hudson Highlands, opposite West Point, in the spring of 1781. The hospital, which was under the charge of Doctor Rush, was at the Robinson House, where Arnold had his headquarters at the time of his treason. Doctor Thacher had been ordered to superintend the operation, and was assisted by Doctors Tomas, Findlay, and myself. There were five hundred patients under treatment at one time, and only four of them died, notwithstanding many of them were improper subjects for the disease. We were compelled to inoculate all, without exception, whatever might be their conditions as to health. Doctor Rush recommended the use of a decoction of the inner bark of the butternut-tree, as a mildly operating cathartic. The country people used it for that purpose. We found it a salutary aid in our treatment."

"Was vaccination practised then?" I inquired.

"Not at all; it was practically unknown in America. Though Doctor Jenner had made his important discovery of the preventative power of vaccination, it was adopted very cautiously by the profession of England, and it was not introduced into London until 1796."

"Did you remain in the medical service in the Continental Army?" I inquired.

"Until after the surrender of Cornwallis," he answered. "I was the surgeon of Colonel Scammell's regiment at the beginning of the siege of Yorktown, and was in constant attendance upon him after he was fatally wounded until his death.[45] Scammell was one of the noblest and bravest of the field officers of the army. You have read how gallantly he behaved at the first battle near Stillwater, where he was wounded. He was very active and very daring.

"As the allied armies approached Yorktown," continued Doctor Munson, "the British retired from their outworks. The American light infantry and some French troops were ordered to take possession of them. As Scammell, the officer of the day, was reconnoitring near a redoubt at the mouth of a little stream near the brink of the river, and was making memoranda of his observations, two or three Hessian horsemen came suddenly upon him and presented their pistols. Perceiving that escape was impossible, he surrendered, saying:

"'Gentlemen, I am your prisoner.'"

Either because they did not understand the colonel's words, or actuated by the want of humanity which so generally characterized these mercenaries, one of them fired, and mortally wounded Scammell. He was carried into Yorktown, where, at the request of

"Gentlemen, I am your prisoner."

Washington, he was paroled and taken to Williamsburg. "I probed the wound," said Doctor Munson, "but could not find the ball. He died on October 6th."

"Did not Colonel Humphreys write an epitaph for his tombstone?" I inquired.

"Yes," replied Doctor Munson, "an appended some elegiac lines, which I distinctly remember."

"Will you please repeat them?" I asked.

"The epitaph was written on the day after the surrender of Cornwallis. The lines referred to were as follows:

'When, though no friend could ward thine early fall,
No guardian angel turn the treacherous ball;
Bless'd shade be soothed! Thy virtues all are known—
Thy fame shall last beyond this moldering stone!
Which conquering armies, from their toils' return,
Read to thy glory, while thy fate they mourn.'

"Nathan Hale, the young martyr of the Revolution, was a pupil at Yale College in your youth. Were you personally acquainted with him?" I asked.

"Oh, yes; he was frequently at my father's house, and he would occasionally have a merry time with me (who was a pretty lively boy) while waiting for my father to come to his study. My father admired young Hale for his manliness, his gentleness, his sobriety, and his intellectual achievements, which marked his course in the college. I was always delighted to hear him talk to my father on scientific subjects. And he had a great taste and a genius for art. He and Major André have often been compared. I am sure he was the equal of André in solid acquirements and many accomplishments, though his junior by eight or ten years."

"What was his personal appearance?" I inquired.

"Truly noble and most attractive," said Doctor Munson. "He was almost six feet in height, perfectly proportioned, and in figure and deportment he was the most manly young man I ever knew. His chest was broad; his muscles were firm; his face wore a most benign expression; his complexion was roseate; his eyes were light blue, and beamed with intelligence; his hair was soft, and light brown in color, and his speech was rather low, deliberate, sweet, and musical. Why, all the girls in New Haven fell in love with him," said Doctor Munson, "and wept tears of real sorrow when they heard of his sad fate. In his dress he was always very neat. He was quick to lend a helping hand to a being in need, whether brute or human. He was continually overflowing with good humor, and was the idol of all his acquaintances."

"Is there a portrait of him in existence?" I asked.

"I never saw one," replied Doctor Munson. "It is said that Mrs. Laurens, Hale's betrothed, who died in Hartford about three years ago, at the age of eighty-eight, had a miniature likeness of him. Hale wrote several letters to father after he left college. I found one of them among his papers after his death. It was written at New London, where Hale was engaged in school teaching. You may read it and copy it, if you desire to," he said, as he took it from a drawer in his old-fashioned "secretary."

The following is a copy of the letter, which was dated "Nov. 30, 1774:"

SIR: I am very happily situated here. I love my employment; find many friends among strangers; have time for scientific studies, and seem to fill the place assigned me with satisfaction. I have a school of more than thirty boys to instruct, about half of them in Latin, and my salary is satisfactory. During the summer I had a morning class of young ladies—about a score—from five to seven o'clock; so you see my time is pretty fully occupied, profitably, I hope, to my pupils and their teacher.

Please accept for yourself and Mrs. Munson the grateful thanks of one who will always remember the kindness he ever experienced whenever he visited your abode.

Your friend,

NATHAN HALE.[46]

"I am delighted," I said, "to hear from the living lips of one who knew Nathan Hale and had met him face to face an account of his person and character, for he was one of the brightest among the 'noble army' of martyrs who died in defence of their faith. Were you at Tappan at the time of the execution of Major André?" I inquired.

"I was, but I never saw the prisoner. My chief, Doctor Thacher, was present at the execution. I have a near neighbor, Nathan Beers, who was one of the guards of Major André while he was in confinement at Tappan. I knew Beers before I entered the army. He was paymaster of Colonel Scammell's regiment at Yorktown. André was respited for one day, you remember. On the morning of the day of his execution he made several pen-

and-ink sketches, among them an outline portrait of himself. His guards, Lieutenant Jabez L. Tomlinson and Sergeant Nathan Beers, were in the room when the sketches were made. André presented the sketch of himself to Lieutenant Tomlinson, who had been very kind and attentive to the prisoner. Tomlinson afterward gave the sketch to his fellow officer, Mr. Beers, and it finally found its way into the Trumbull gallery of Yale College, where it may be seen."

"Mr. Beers must be a very aged man," I said. "Would a call upon him by a stranger be an intrusion or an infliction of discomfort?" I asked.

"He is nearly one hundred years old," said Doctor Munson, "and his mental faculties are totally wrecked. An interview would be fruitless of any information; nevertheless, if seeing him, as an interesting relic of soldiers of the Revolution, would be a gratification to you, I will go with you to his house, which is only a few doors away in this street. I am one of the few persons whom he recognizes at sight."

"It would be a great gratification," I replied.

We called at the residence of Mr. Beers. One of the family welcomed Doctor Munson cordially at the door, and after sitting a few minutes in the parlor we were taken to another room, in which the venerable man was sitting in an easy chair. He extended his attenuated hand and said, "How d' do, doctor?" Then he took my hand and motioned us to a seat.

Mr. Beers's scanty locks were perfectly white; the luster of his eyes had departed; his face was very thin and wrinkled; his voice was feeble, and his once powerful frame seemed almost like a shadow. I looked with reverence upon that silent wreck of one of the truest patriots of the old war for independence, and an honest man, "the noblest work of God." Doctor Munson had told me, in brief, of some points of his personal history. By misfortune he became involved in debt, and struggled with poverty and privations for many years. At length Congress allowed his claim for a pension for services as paymaster in the Continental Army, and he received arrearages to the amount of several thousand dollars—sufficient for a competence during his life; but he turned over a greater portion of it to his creditors. Mr. Beers died a few months after my visit, at the age of about ninety-eight years.

That visit to Mr. Beers was one of the most impressive incidents of my life. I was brought face to face with living men who had personally known and conversed with the two most notable and patriotic spies of the Revolution. I say *patriotic*, for both Hale and André were ardently devoted to the interests of their respective countries. There was a difference in the quality of that devotion. That of the British spy was mingled with personal considerations; that of the American spy had no alloy of that kind. André avowed that in the enterprise in which he was engaged all he sought "was military glory, the applause of his King and country, and perhaps a brigadiership." His last words were (addressed to the American officers present), "I request you, gentlemen, that you will bear me witness to the world that I die like a brave man."

Hale had said, "I wish to be useful. If the exigencies of my country demand a peculiar service, its claims to the performance of that service are imperious." His last words were, "I only regret that I have but one life to lose for my country!"

Chapter XIX
The Rescued Baby

In the summer of 1781 efforts were made by the British military authorities in New York and in Canada to seize the persons of distinguished citizens in the State of New York, in order to hold them as hostages or for exchange. General Philip Schuyler and Governor George Clinton were specially designated for such attempts. Armed parties were sent out of the city stealthily for such purposes, and Tories in the interior were so employed.

The person of General Schuyler was particularly coveted. He was not only the foremost man in the State in the extent of his influence, but was then a member of the Continental Congress and one of the most trustworthy officers in the service of his country. He had been the efficient commander of the Northern Department in opposing and checking the British invasion of New York from Canada in 1777, until he was displaced by the intrigues of men in and out of Congress. He was now out of the military service, and was living at his elegant home in the southern suburbs of the city of Albany, but was actively engaged in assisting the General Government in its financial operations and in providing supplies for the armies. In these labors he was the most trusted and efficient assistant of Robert Morris, who had lately been appointed Superintendent of Finance, or Secretary of the Treasury. So vigilant was Schuyler at all times in the public service, that he was called the "Eye of the Northern Department." On his retirement from the army he was furnished with a guard of six soldiers for the protection of his person. At the time we are considering, Schuyler was employed by Washington in intercepting communications between General Sir Henry Clinton, in New York, and General Sir Frederick Haldimand, the Governor-General of Canada.

The munificent rewards that were secretly offered by the British for the seizure of prominent persons, and the promise of plunder, had excited the cupidity of the Tories in the vicinity of Albany. Several seizures had been attempted, and some had been accomplished by them. Among the boldest of the leading Tories in active service was John Walter Meyer, a colleague of the notorious marauder, Joe Bettys.[47] He was employed to abduct General Schuyler. Accompanied by a gang of Tories, Canadians, and Indians, he repaired to the neighborhood of Albany, but uncertain how well General Schuyler might be guarded, he lurked among the pine shrubbery in the vicinity for eight or ten days. He seized a Dutch laborer, and learned from him the exact position of affairs at Schuyler's house; and extorting an oath of secrecy from the man, he let him go. The Dutchman appears to have made a mental reservation, for he gave Schuyler information of his experience. A loyalist, who was the general's personal friend and was cognizant of Walter Meyer's designs, also gave him warning. Thus forewarned, the general and his family were constantly vigilant, and the guards were kept continually on duty, three at a time.

At the close of a sultry day in August General Schuyler and his family were sitting in the font hall of the mansion. The servants were dispersed about the premises. The three guards, retired for the night, were asleep in the basement room of the house, and the three who were on duty, oppressed by the heat, were lying on the cool grass in the garden. A servant announced to the general that a stranger desired to speak to him at the back gate. The stranger's errand was at once comprehended. The doors of the house were immediately shut and close-barred. The family were hastily collected in an upper room, and the general ran to his bedchamber for his arms. From the window he saw the house surrounded by armed men. For the purpose of arousing the guards on the grass, and perchance to alarm the town, he fired a pistol from the window.

The assailants burst open the doors. At the same moment Mrs. Schuyler perceived that in the confusion and retreat from the hall, her infant child, only a few months old, had been left in the cradle in the nursery below. Parental love subdued all fear, and the mother was flying to the rescue of her babe, when her husband interfered and prevented her. Her life was of more consequence than that of the infant. Their third daughter, afterward the wife of Stephen Van Rensselaer (the Albany patron), rushed down the two flights of stairs, snatched the still sleeping infant from the cradle, and flew with it toward the great lower staircase. One of the Indians hurled a sharp tomahawk at the flying girl, but it affected no other harm than a slight cut in her dress a few inches from the head of the babe and a wound in the mahogany rail of the staircase where it struck. At the stairs she met Walter Meyer, who, supposing her to be a servant, exclaimed:

"Wench, wench! Where is your master?"

With great presence of mind the courageous sister answered:

"Gone to alarm the town."

The Tory leader's followers were in the dining-room stealing the silver plate and other valuables. He called them together for consultation. At that moment the general threw up a window, and, as if speaking to numbers, called out in a loud voice:

"Come on, my brave fellows! Surround the house and secure the villains who are plundering!"

The assailants made a precipitate retreat, carrying with them the three guards who were in the house and a large quantity of silver plate.

The bursting open of the doors of the house had aroused the sleeping guards in the basement room, who rushed up to the back hall where they had left their arms, but their weapons were gone. Mrs. Church, a married daughter of General Schuyler, who was there at the time, without a suspicion that they might be wanted, had removed the arms just before the attack, on account of apprehended injury to her little boy, whom she had found playing with them. The guards had no other weapons but their brawny fists, and these they used manfully until they were overpowered. They were taken to Canada; and when they were exchanged and had returned, General Schuyler gave each of them a farm in Saratoga. Their names were John Tubbs, John Corlies, and John Ward. The marauders fled with their booty to Canada.

In the summer of 1848 I visited friends at Oswego, then a pleasant village on the southern shore of Lake Ontario, at the mouth of the Oswego River. I was informed that a daughter of General Schuyler, his youngest child, and wife of Major James Cochran, a nephew of

"One of the Indians hurled a sharp tomahawk at the flying girl."

the general, was living in the village. My friends spoke of her as a most charming old lady, almost seventy years of age, who was beloved by everybody who knew her because of the sweetness of her disposition, the blamelessness of her life, her abounding kindness toward the needy and afflicted, her social graces, and her intellectual gifts.

At a suitable hour I called on the venerable couple. Major Cochran was almost four-score years old, feeble in bodily health, but mentally vigorous. He was a son of Doctor John Cochran, Surgeon-General of the Middle Department of the Continental Army, who married a sister of General Schuyler. The major himself was a member of Congress during the administration of the elder President Adams. His family relationship and his position gave him opportunities to become acquainted with most of the general officers of the Revolution, and the utterances of his reminiscences of persons and events of the long-buried past gave me great pleasure and edification during our brief interview.

Major Cochran related the amusing circumstances of his nomination and election as a member of Congress (1797–99). A vessel was to be launched on Seneca Lake, at Geneva. It being an unusual event, the people gathered there from far and near to witness it. The young people determined to have a dance at night. A fiddle was found, but a fiddler was lacking. Young Cochran, who was present, was an amateur performer on the violin, and his services were demanded on that occasion. He gratified the joyous company, and at the supper table a gentleman remarked, in commendation of his achievement, "He is fit for Congress." The hint was favorably received by the company. The matter was "talked up,"

and he was nominated for and elected to a seat in Congress from the district which then included the whole of New York west of Schenectady.

"So, you see," said Major Cochran, with a pleasant smile, as he finished the story, "I fiddled my way into Congress."

The major died a few months after my visit.

Mrs. Cochran was ten years the junior of her husband. She was tall and slender, graceful in figure, with rather deep-set and exceedingly expressive eyes, and good-humor and benevolence pervading her whole countenance. She told me of her home life at Albany; of the eminent persons she had met there in her childhood and young womanhood; of the domestic character of her father, and of the sweet face and abounding goodness of her mother "toward everybody," whose maiden name in full—Catharine Van Rensselaer—she bore. These seemed to constitute her happiest memories. She spoke with enthusiasm of the broad Christian charity and kindly hospitality of her father, displayed toward friends and enemies during the war, which she knew only by testimony from the lips of others, for she was born in 1781. She spoke of his unswerving patriotism under cruel persecutions and grave affronts, and of his fortitude and patience while tortured with hereditary gout when in the military service, and of the perils which surrounded him at times from the Tories, who, stimulated by the prospect of great rewards, sought to carry him off a prisoner to the British at New York City.

I told Mrs. Cochran in brief the story I had recently heard of the attempt of Walter Meyer to abduct her father, and the narrow escape from death of the rescued baby. I observed that her countenance beamed with an amused expression while I related the incident, and when I concluded the narrative her smile developed into hearty laughter, as she exclaimed:

"Why, *I* am that rescued baby!"

I was silenced.

"Yes," she said, "I am that rescued baby. It was I who was sleeping in that cradle in the nursery when Sister Peggy snatched me from it and ran upstairs with me. She was Sister Margaret, who married the Patroon Van Rensselaer. If you ever visit my father's house at Albany—and I hope you will—you may see the scar of the wound which the Indian's tomahawk inflicted on the stair-rail."

"I have something curious to tell you about the silver plate which was carried off at that time," said Major Cochran. "I have been informed that Lieutenant-Colonel Barry St. Leger, whose headquarters were at Montreal at that time, and who was carrying on a sort of guerilla warfare, received an intimation from Governor Haldimand that the seizure of General Schuyler was very desirable. St. Leger proposed a plan which the governor sanctioned. He sent out a scout on pretence of making observations, but with secret instructions to penetrate to Albany and attempt the abduction of General Schuyler. A portion of the scout was a band of Tories led by Walter Meyer, and to him was entrusted the task of seizing the general. He attempted it with a motley gang, with the result which you have related.

"General Schuyler afterward wrote a courteous letter to St. Leger, complaining of the plunder of his house by troops under his command, and asking for a return of the plate. St. Leger replied as courteously, and assured General Schuyler that the circumstance had mortified him, and that the moment he heard of it he did everything in his power 'to rescue from the hands of a scoundrelly silversmith what had escaped the disfiguration of his crucible, and which is now in my possession.' The plate was never returned. One of the articles rescued from the crucible was a soup tureen. And here comes in the curious part of my story," said Major Cochran. "I was at Washington in 1841, on the occasion of the inauguration of President Harrison, and while in the rotunda of the Capitol, viewing Trumbull's picture of the surrender of Burgoyne, a stranger at my elbow inquired:

"'Who is that fine-looking man in the group of citizen's dress?'

"'General Schuyler,' I replied.

"'General Schuyler!' repeated the stranger; 'why, I ate soup not long ago at Bellville, in Canada, from a silver tureen that was carried off from his house by some Tories in the Revolution.'

"This was the first and only time any of his family ever heard of the plundered article, excepting the letter of St. Leger."

I visited Mrs. Cochran twice during her widowhood, the last time at the beginning of August 1857. She then seemed to be in fairly good health, but the Angel of Death was hovering near, and she departed from earth before the close of that month. She was the last living child of General Philip Schuyler.

Chapter XX
The Spy of the Neutral Ground

Soon after the publication of my *Pictorial Field Book of the Revolution*, I received a note from the eminent physician and scholar, the late Doctor John W. Francis, saying:

"Come to my house this evening and meet an old friend of mine, who wishes to see you and tell you something about Enoch Crosby."

I was entrusted to Mr. M—, a venerable gentleman, who said he had read my work with much interest, for in his young manhood he had known some men and women of the Revolution. "Indeed," he said, "I was one of the boys of the period, for I was born in 1770, and am eighty-two years old."

I thanked him for his kind intentions to give me trustworthy information about Enoch Crosby, who appears almost like a myth in history and romance.

"I observe," he said, "that in writing of Enoch Crosby as the original Harvey Birch of Cooper's novel, *The Spy*, you allude to doubts having been cast upon that identity. I will tell you what *I* know about Enoch Crosby, personally and from my father, who was his neighbor and friend. Why, I have no more doubt of Enoch Crosby being the original of Harvey Birch than I have of my own existence. Captain Barnum's little book, to which you allude, I believe to be true, every word of it, sir."

"But Mr. Cooper makes a declaration that puzzles me," I said. "In the summer of 1850 I wrote to Mr. Cooper and inquired about the trustworthiness of Barnum's narrative. To my surprise, he replied that he had never seen the book, though it had been dedicated to him almost a quarter of a century before; also, that he never heard the name of Enoch Crosby uttered before he wrote *The Spy*, in 1820, nor since, until it was coupled with his Harvey Birch. He referred me to the introduction to the revised edition of *The Spy*, then recently published."

"I have read that introduction," said Mr. M—, "and it confirms my conviction of the identity of Harvey Birch and Enoch Crosby. He tells us as plainly as if he had spoken the words, that John Jay, who was chairman of the Committee of Safety, related the 'anecdote' to which he refers. Jay was, of course, in honor bound not to mention the *name* of the secret agent he had employed, for the character of a spy is held to be disreputable, though it may be a patriotic one."

"Did you know Enoch Crosby personally?" I inquired.

"Yes. We resided near the Westchester and Putnam County line, not far from the Crosby homestead, where the patriotic hero dwelt. His wife was a distant relation of my

father, and Crosby visited us frequently when I was a young man. I was always delighted by listening to his stories of adventure during the war, as given long years afterward by Captain Barnum. When I was more than fifty years of age, in business in this city, I read Cooper's *Spy* aloud to my aged father, at my house, and we continually remarked, 'Harvey Birch resembled Enoch Crosby so much!' And when Captain Barnum's book was published we recognized a truthful record of many of the incidents in the career of Crosby which we had heard from his own lips.

"I distinctly remember," continued Mr. M—, "that while on a visit with my father at his country home, soon after Barnum's little book appeared, I rode with him to Bedford to see Mr. Jay on some business. It was a beautiful spring day. We found the venerable statesman sitting on the piazza of his pleasant mansion near a budding wistaria vine. He knew my father well. In the course of their conversation my father referred to Barnum's book. Mr. Jay had not seen it. When my father observed that 'it made the then venerable Enoch Crosby the reality of the fictitious Harvey Birch,' the old gentleman smiled and said:

"'Enoch Crosby did noble service in the war. He was as bold as a lion and as cunning as a fox. Cooper has certainly told much in *The Spy* of what I knew of Crosby's doings. But on that subject I desire to neither affirm nor deny.

"This remark of course closed the conversation on that subject."

"When did you last see Enoch Crosby?" I inquired.

"In his extreme old age. He was called as a witness in a court held at our City Hall, about 1827, I think. The newspapers had already coupled his name with that of Harvey Birch. An old gentleman who was in the courtroom, and had known Crosby quite intimately, but supposed he was dead, recognized him before the opening of the court, and they had mutual greetings. After Crosby had testified, his old friend introduced him to the audience as the original of Harvey Birch. Crosby was instantly made famous, for the newspapers mentioned this incident in the courtroom.

"Cooper's *Spy*," continued Mr. M—, "had lately been dramatized. The manager of one of the theatres invited Mr. Crosby to attend a performance two evenings afterward, when *The Spy* was specially presented for that occasion. Notice had been given that the real spy would be present. The house was crowded. Mr. Crosby was introduced to the audience as Harvey Birch, when he was saluted with rounds of applause and the waving of handkerchiefs."

"Well do I remember the scene," said Doctor Francis, "for I was present. Greatly interested, I called on Crosby the next day at Washington Hall, on the corner of Broadway and Chambers Street, when he told me that he recognized in the play some of his own performances nearly fifty years before. He then seemed to be in robust health. His figure was nearly six feet in height, and erect, his shoulders were broad, and his mind was vigorous. He told me he was eighty-one years of age."

Mr. M— related several stirring incidents in the career of Enoch Crosby as a spy not mentioned by Barnum. I bade him adieu at ten o'clock, much gratified and edified by the interview.

Enoch Crosby's adventures as recorded in the third person by Captain Barnum were related by his own lips to the compiler. I can give here only a brief account of a few of them.

Crosby was a native of Massachusetts. When he was a little child his parents settled in the southeastern part of (present) Putnam Co., N.Y. His father was a stanch Whig, and as Enoch grew to young manhood his patriotism was stimulated by the events which immediately preceded the old war for independence. He was a lusty youth; learned the trade of a shoemaker, and when the war broke out he entered the army destined to invade Canada in 1775. He sickened on Lake Champlain, and went no farther.

Westchester Co. abounded with Tories, and in time became a neutral ground, scourged by marauders from both armies. When his health was restored Crosby left his home to join a detachment of the army at Verplanck's Point. In a lonely place, just toward dusk on a warm day in September, he fell in with an apparent gentleman, whom he soon discovered to be a Tory. Crosby immediately conceived a plan for the benefit of his country. He pretended to be a loyalist on his way to join the British army at New York. The gentleman invited him to tarry all night at his house, saying several of his neighbors were nearly ready to "go down," and that it would be safer for him to go with them than alone. Crosby readily assented. The next day he was introduced to several of these young Tories, and met a large number of them at their usual rendezvous that night. He learned their names, residences, and plans. Pretending to be anxious to reach New York speedily, he departed alone, went to White Plains, and revealed his discoveries to the Committee of Safety sitting there—Messrs. Jay, Platt, Duer, and Sackett. At their request he piloted a party of Rangers to the nest of Tories which he had just left, by whom they were all arrested and taken to White Plains Jail.

The committee perceiving how useful Crosby might be as an informer, employed him as a secret agent for the discovery of Tories and their plans, agreeing to do all in their power to protect him from harm. Equipping himself with a peddler's pack filled with a shoemaker's "kit," he started out on his perilous quest in the disguise of a mechanic seeking work.

Crosby's first adventure was not far away. Just at sunset he was at the door of a farmhouse craving entertainment for the night. The farmer's wife, suspicious of everybody in those troublesome times, hesitated. Inquiring what was in his pack, Crosby told her he was a shoemaker, when she said he might stay long enough to make her John a pair of shoes. Crosby, shrewdly suspecting he was among Tories, told her he was on his way to the British army to make shoes for the soldiers, and that they were then approaching White Plains. She was delighted, and when her husband came in she told him the good news. He greeted Crosby warmly, and he was entertained as a friend of the royal cause. The next day he was introduced to the captain of a company nearly ready to join the British, and was shown by him a long muster-roll. Crosby became the guest of the captain that night, who revealed to his new recruit all their plans.

Retiring early, when all was quiet Crosby left his bed, sped to White Plains, revealed his discovery, and returned before daybreak. On the following night the company were all assembled at the captain's house. Crosby was one of the most active among them. Suddenly a tramp of horses was heard, and then a shout at the door:

"Surrender, or you are all dead men!"

Some fled to the attic, some to the cellar, but all were arrested, taken to White Plains, and then sent up the Hudson and imprisoned in the Dutch church at Fishkill village, five miles from the landing. Crosby was among the prisoners, who were taken before the Committee of Safety, sitting at a house near Fishkill village. When left alone with the committee, after the other prisoners were taken away, a plan for his escape was formed, and he was instructed as to his movements after he should escape. He was to go to a person at Wappinger's Creek, who would give him directions about service on the west side of the Hudson. Then he was to assume the name of John Brown.

On that night Crosby passed out of a window of the church, adroitly avoiding the sentinels. He fled to a swamp and baffled pursuers.

The committee had been informed that a British officer was secretly recruiting a company of Tories for the royal army, not far north of Newburgh. Thither Crosby was sent. He sought employment as a shoemaker at a farmhouse, and was engaged to work on the farm a few days. He tried in vain to elicit from the farmer any indications of his politics. At length, while in the field, they heard the booming of cannon below. After some conversation Crosby said:

"What do you think of all this business?"

The answer revealed the Tory proclivities of the farmer. Crosby led him on. He expressed to the farmer his desire to join the British army if he could. Satisfied with evidences of the laborer's loyalty, the farmer told him that in a mountain not far off was a cave, used as headquarters by a British captain, and who would be glad to receive him as a recruit, with whom he could go in safety to New York. That night the farmer piloted Crosby to the cave, where he was cordially received. He told the captain the story of his escape from the rebels at Fishkill, joined his company as John Brown, and gained the full confidence of his commander.

An arrangement was made for a general rendezvous of the company at a barn near Cornwall, at a certain time, to prepare for proceeding to the British lines. Crosby now wished to send a communication to the Committee of Safety. To be absent from headquarters long might excite suspicion. He shrewdly suggested to the captain that Townsend's Rangers were ubiquitous, and if they should fall upon them at the barn they might ruin the whole corps. He proposed a partial scattering of the band until the hour for departure. The captain assented, when Crosby repaired to the house of a stanch Whig, whom he knew, and desired him to saddle his horse and carry a message to the committee at Fishkill. It was done. Crosby wrote:

GENTLEMEN: I hasten this express to request you to order Captain Townsend's company of Rangers to repair immediately to the barn on the west side of Butter Hill, and there to secret themselves until we arrive, which will be to-morrow evening, probably about seven o'clock, where, with about thirty Tories, they may find your obedient servant,

JOHN BROWN.

Accompanied by Colonel Duer, one of the Committee of Safety, Captain Townsend with his Rangers appeared promptly at the appointed time and place, and secured the whole band of Tories, with the English captain. Duer had come to protect Crosby, for Townsend, chagrined at his escape from Fishkill, might now use him harshly. They were all taken to Fishkill. Crosby was marched a mile from the church to a farmhouse, where Jay, one of the committee, resided, and which was the temporary headquarters of Townsend. The latter, determined that his troublesome prisoner should not escape, put Crosby in a room by himself under a strong guard.

At about midnight Crosby was awakened by a gentle touch, and saw the sweet face of a maiden bending over him with a dark lantern.

"Follow me without speaking," she said.

Crosby obeyed. As they left the room the girl locked the door, led Crosby out by a back way, and pointing to a mountain which lay bathed in moonlight, bade him seek safety among its crags.

"But how have you effected this?" asked the bewildered prisoner, "and what will be the result to yourself and that careless sentinel?"

"Fear nothing for either," replied the girl, "but hasten to the mountains. I shall instantly return the key to Townsend's pocket. Dr. Miller's opiates are wonderfully powerful when mixed with brandy! Now fly for your life! The sentinel shall be on his feet when the relief comes. You have not a moment to lose. I shall be at Hopewell by the time the alarm is given. Not another word—I want no thanks—Jay is your protector. Fly!"

Townsend and his men had fasted all day. The maiden provided the captain and the sentinel with a bountiful supper, and with plenty of brandy, which she had drugged, and they slept soundly until morning. Townsend was puzzled. How could the prisoner escape

"Follow me without speaking," she said.

from the locked room, and the key in his (the captain's) pocket? He concluded he had climbed up the chimney. He swore that if he ever caught Crosby again he would hang him on the spot!

The Tories finally suspected Crosby of being, as he was, their secret enemy, and he was more frequently placed in very perilous positions than before. His frequent mysterious escapes when with them he was made a prisoner, and some other incidents, so satisfied them that he was a Whig spy, that they resolved to destroy him. Crosby perceived the rising storm, and resolved to seek shelter from it. He retired to the house of his brother-in-law, in the Hudson Highlands, and kept within doors most of the time. One night an armed gang came to his retreat and broke into his room. He was awakened from a sound sleep by a large, rough-visaged man with a light in one hand and a pistol in the other. Crosby leaped from his bed, but before he could reach his gun the man discharged his pistol at him, but without effect. Crosby grappled with his antagonist, laid him on the floor, and held him with a tight grasp. Three other men came to the assistance of their comrade. Two of them held Crosby's arms, while a third presented a pistol to his breast.

"Don't shoot the rascal!" exclaimed one of them. "Let us pound him to death!"

They began the operation, when Crosby fought desperately with his fists and feet. At length, exhausted by exertion and loss of blood, he fell on the floor insensible. Supposing him to be dead, they plundered the house and fled.

Finding it no longer prudent to play the perilous part of a spy, Crosby abandoned the secret service, and became a subordinate officer in a light infantry corps organized and disciplined by Lafayette. It was regarded as the finest body of soldiers in the Continental Army. After reviewing it, Washington formally presented it to the young marquis, who was so delighted that he gave to each of its officers an elegant sword, and to each of the private soldiers a beautiful uniform, at his own expense.

A detachment of this corps served for a while under the command of Colonel Van Cortlandt, on the Neutral Ground. While Crosby, at the head of a small detachment, was on duty on Teller's Point, a British sloop-of-war anchored off the promontory. With an unconquerable love for stratagem, and a desire, as he said, for a "little fun for his soldiers," he played a successful trick. Accompanied by six men, he went to the verge of the wooded point, and while five of his men concealed themselves in the woods, the sixth man showed himself conspicuously in Lafayette's uniform. Very soon eleven men in a boat went from the sloop to the shore to catch the Yankee, who as they approached fled to the woods, pursued by the Britons. So soon as they had passed his own little party, Crosby exclaimed:

"Come on, my boys! Now we have them!"

Every man sprang up with a shout, took every Briton prisoner, and the next day marched them to Fishkill, and confined them in the Dutch church there.

At the close of the war Crosby became a small farmer. He was twice married, was justice of the peace twenty-eight years, and was a deacon of a Presbyterian Church many years. He died in the town of Southeast, in Putnam Co., on January 26th, 1834, in the eighty-eighth year of his age.

Chapter XXI
An Artist's Reminiscences—The Last Battle of the Revolution

Doctor Alexander Anderson, who died in January, 1870, at the age of nearly ninety-five years, was the pioneer wood-engraver in America. He retained his mental faculties almost impaired until the end of his days on the earth, and his physical vigor was quite as remarkable. I have in my possession the last block upon which he exercised his artistic skill. On it is a pencil drawing by his own hand, about one half engraved; the remained is covered with protecting tissue paper, from which he had cut fragments as the work progressed. He left it unfinished three months before his death.

I knew Doctor Anderson intimately for thirty years, and from the well of his experience with the bucket of a most tenacious memory I drew copious draughts of information concerning long-past events in the city of New York, where he was born and resided for ninety years.

Doctor Anderson's father was a Scotchman and a printer. He was a social and political friend of Isaac Sears—"King Sears," as he was called—one of the foremost leaders of the "Sons of Liberty" in New York when the old war for independence was a-kindling. They were neighbors, living near Beekman's Slip, East River, and there our artist was born, two days after the fight at Lexington, in the spring of 1775. His father published a small Whig newspaper entitled the *Constitutional Gazette*. He had printed many of the handbills calling meetings of the people "at the Liberty Pole," or in "The Fields," now the City Hall Park. He offended and annoyed the Tories, who called him "John Anderson the Rebel," and long years afterward one of them, also a Scotchman, said to our artist:

"I knew your father weel. A line at the head of his paper read, 'Printed by John Anderson, Beekman Slip: Price, Two Coppers,' and these were the only words of truth in it."

After the battle on Long Island, in August, 1776, and the British army were menacing the city of New York with capture, the Whig journalist thought it prudent to fly from the doomed town with his family, his household goods, his type, and his press. He barely escaped capture by pickets of the British army, which had crossed the East River far up the island; and he had reached Harlem Heights on his way to the mainland, when his wagons were seized for the use of the patriot forces; their contents were thrown out, and Anderson's papers and books were used for making cartridges by the garrison at Fort Washington. He escaped to Greenwich, in Connecticut, where his wife and their two infant boys were cared for by friends, while the father engaged as a scout for the patriot army in Westchester County. After the proclamation of peace he returned to the city, hired a house near the foot of Murray Street, not far from the North River, and resumed the business of printing, but not of publishing.

Young Anderson displayed a taste and genius for art, particularly engraving, at a very early period of his life. He first used copper and type-metal for the purpose. Engraving on wood was then unknown in America. Bewick, the great reformer of the art in England, was then astonishing the public by the beauty of his woodcut illustrations, especially of natural history. Young Anderson saw some of them in Durell's book-store, and then learned for the first time that they were done on boxwood, the best material still in use for wood-engravings. He was then making illustrations for an edition of *The Looking-Glass for the Mind*, and had finished about one half of them on type-metal. He tried wood, succeeded, and made the remainder on that material. The writer possesses two of these original blocks, which, with the unfinished engraving of 1867, displays the pioneer's work done at periods seventy-five years apart.

Meanwhile young Anderson had studied medicine and graduated at the Medical School of Columbia College. His thesis on that occasion was "Chronic Mania," the doctrine of which, then first promulgated in due form, has ever since been accepted by the medical profession as correct. He preferred the practice of the graphic art to the healing art, and pursued both simultaneously. Conscientious, and reverent of parental wishes, he was assiduous in his attentions to the sick at their homes and in the hospital during the prevalence of the yellow-fever in New York in 1798. That fearful scourge bereft him of father, mother, wife, infant son, brother, sister, mother-in-law, and sister-in-law, and many dear friends, whom he attended in their illness. Like Job, he was utterly desolated, yet, with the sublime faith and equanimity which never forsook him, he allowed no murmur to escape his lips.

Doctor Anderson had a vivid recollection of the "Doctors' Mob," the most exciting event in the history of the city since the evacuation by the British and Tories. He was then a lad thirteen years old. The mob was the creation of rumor. The citizens had been much excited by the fact the graves in the Potter's Field (now Washington Square), in the Negro burying-ground between Chambers and Reade streets, east of Broadway, and in several churchyards had been robbed of their recent occupants. Suspicion was directed toward the hospital on Broadway—the only one in the city—as the recipient of the stolen bodies. One day a thoughtless student exhibited to some boys playing near by a limb from a body he was engaged in dissecting. They told the story. Rumors that the bodies from the rifled graves were certainly at the hospital spread rapidly over the city, and very soon an excited multitude appeared before the building and broke into it, clamoring loudly for the doctors, and destroying some fine anatomical specimens. The terrified physicians could not escape, and they would have been murdered by the mob had not the city authorities rescued them and placed them in the jail in the Park for the safety of their persons. The excited populace, foiled, became comparatively quiet, but the riot was renewed the next morning, when Colonel Hamilton, John Jay, and others addressed the mob with soothing words. The orators were pelted with bricks and stones. The disturbance continued all day, and toward evening it became so alarming that the mayor (Duane) came with a body of militia to suppress it. Again the rioters were addressed by two or three citizens, and were answered by flying missiles from the hands of the mob. While the Baron Von Steuben was trying to mediate, and begging the mayor not to order the militia to fire on the mob until every other measure should fail, a flying stone prostrated him. That changed his views of the situation. As he rose to his feet, it is said, he exclaimed:

"Fire, mayor, fire!"

The militia did so at once, when five rioters were killed, several were wounded, and the remainder were dispersed. Speaking of the scene one day, Dr. Anderson said to me:

"I ought to remember it, for my brother and I were standing near the Baron Von Stueben when he was knocked down by a stone thrown by a rioter, and a small one hit my leg. The mayor also was hit, but was not much hurt."

"I suppose you saw President Washington quite often in New York," I remarked, in conversation with the doctor one day.

"Only a few times," he replied. "I was a youngster in the crowd on Broad and Wall streets at the ceremony of his inauguration, but could get only a few glimpses of him as he stood in the outside gallery of the Federal Hall, for the men and women in the street were so large, and I was so small [never much over five feet five inches in height]. Once I saw the President and Mrs. Washington come out of St. Paul's Church, and also out of his house in Cherry Street and get into his carriage. Twice I saw him riding in his fine English coach with Mrs. Washington and the Custis children. It was pleasant weather, and the blinds were opened."

"Did you ever see Citizen Genet?" I inquired.[48]

"Many times," he answered. "You know, he married Governor Clinton's daughter and lived in this city. He was a good-looking, medium-sized Frenchman, of courteous manners, and very quick in his movements and speech. His head resembled that of Tom Paine in shape, particularly his receding forehead. He had a large aquiline nose and piercing dark eyes. I saw him land at the Battery when he came from Philadelphia, a representative of the French Republic. There was a great hubbub at his landing—cannon-firing, drum-beating, and wild huzzaing. A grand procession with bands of music received him and escorted him to the Coffee House near the foot of Wall Street. I was then eighteen years old, and took much interest in politics. The two parties, Federalists and Republicans, abused each other most shamefully. The Republicans blamed Washington for issuing his famous proclamation of neutrality, for they wanted to help the French revolutionists. They almost worshipped Genet. They wore the French tri-colored cockade on their hats; and that night the Marsellaise Hymn was sung in the streets. My father was a Federalist, and of course so was I. On the day after Genet's arrival I went to a gathering on Broadway, near Maiden Lane, and heard Colonel Troup, a Federalist, make a speech in commendation of Washington's proclamation. Several resolutions of the same tenor were adopted."

"You spoke of Tom Paine; did you ever see him?" I inquired.

"No, not in life. I went with John Wesley Jarvis, the painter, to Paine's lodgings in Grove Street on the day of his death, and assisted that artist in taking a plaster cast of his face, which is now in collection of the New York Historical Society."

"Have you any recollections of the evacuation of New York by the British?" I asked.

"Not much," he replied, "for I was only between eight and nine years old then—eight in April, and that was late in November, you know. I have a very particular remembrance of one event of that day," he continued. "I saw the whole of the last battle of the Revolution. It was fought in New York."

"Tell me the story, if you please," I said.

"It is but a short one," he replied. "When we came back to the city after the proclamation of peace, my father hired a house near the foot of Murray Street, near the corner of Greenwich Street. There were then very few houses between ours and Broadway, and pasture-lots were near us. Opposite ours was a boarding-house kept by Benjamin Day. His wife was really the proprietor. She was a comely, stout-built woman, about forty years old, and was of a Dutch family at Hackensack, N.J. She was an ardent Whig, and possessed a brave heart and a stubborn will. She could never conceal her opinions, and many a bout she had with her tongue among her Tory neighbors. The British, you may remember, claimed the right of possession of the city until noon on the day fixed for the evacuation. It was conceded by the Americans, and the troops under Washington and Governor Clinton and other civil officers halted at Chatham Square and beyond until the British began to move toward their shipping at a little past noon. Mrs. Day's patriotism was too intense and her job too impatient to allow her to wait until noon to give them visible expression. So as soon as she breakfasted that morning she raised the American flag on a pole which she had planted in front of her dwelling in anticipation of the great event of the day. About nine o'clock in the morning, a bright and frosty one, I was sitting on the porch of our house in the sunshine, enjoying the sight of the beautiful flag waving in a gentle breeze, when I saw a burly, red faced British officer, in full uniform and unattended, walking rapidly down the street. Mrs. Day was quietly sweeping in front of her house, and casting a glance of satisfaction now and then toward her floating flag, when the officer, half out of breath, halted before her. In a loud and angry tone and coarse, rough voice, and pointing toward the Stars and Stripes, he demanded:

"'Who hoisted that rebel flag?'

"Mrs. Day stopped sweeping, and confronting the rude inquirer with a scornful frown, said in a firm voice, made more vehement by her indignation:

"'It is not a rebel flag, sir, but the flag of a free people. Who are you?'

"'Pull down that flag!' roared the red-faced Briton in a rage, 'or you'll find out to your cost who I am.'

"'Who *are* you?' again inquired Mrs. Day.

"'I'm his Majesty's provost-marshal, charged not to allow a rebel flag to fly in this town before noon to-day. Pull down that flag!'

"'I will not do it,' said Mrs. Day firmly, keeping her eyes fixed on the glowing face of the angry officer. 'I raised that flag with my own hands. If the King himself stood where you do and commanded me to pull it down, I wouldn't do it.'

"'You cursed rebel in petticoats!' exclaimed the officer. 'If you were not a woman I'd hang you on the spot. That rebel rag *shall* come down!'

"He seized the halyards, when Mrs. Day sprang forward like a roused tigress, and with her broom struck the intruder upon the head with heavy and rapid blows. His hat went off at the first blow, and she made the powder fly from his wig. I saw it glisten in the sunlight like a little spray. A brutal nature is always a cowardly one. As the man in the window shouted 'hurrah!' lustily, and the woman's weapon was not at rest a moment, the burly Briton, no doubt believing that prudence is the better part of valor, released his hold of the halyards, snatched up his hat from the ground, and moved off as rapidly as he came, muttering curses. Mrs. Day was left the valiant mistress of her castle, and her banner waving in triumph. I clapped my little hands as loudly as I could as Mrs. Day started for her house, a victor in the last battle of the Revolution. At her door she turned and dropped a courtesy."

"Do you know who her antagonist was?" I inquired.

"The man who saw the whole affair from the window told my father that he was Bill Cunningham, the infamous provost-marshal who treated the American prisoners in New York so cruelly, selling the rations that were provided for them, putting the money in his own pocket, and allowing them to starve to death.[49] It is said that when he was on a scaffold, in England, and about to be hung for some crime, he was filled with remorse, and confessed to the attending priest that he had thus murdered fully two thousand American prisoners at New York.

"That rebel rag shall come down."

"When my father came home at sunset he was in high spirits. He had seen the last British transport sail out upon the ocean, never to return. The British, to avoid seeing their flag hauled down from the staff at Fort George, on the Battery, had nailed it fast and slushed the pole, that it might not be climbed. But it was climbed by a brave youth, who nailed cleats on the flagstaff as he ascended it, so forming a ladder. He tore down the British flag and put the Stars and Stripes in its place while some of the British ships were yet within the Narrows. When he heard the story of Mrs. Day's victory, and that I saw the fight, he said, 'Aleck, never forget it.' I never have forgotten it."

Notes

Chapter I

1. Major Barrett was a grandson of Colonel James Barrett, a Provincial officer in the French and Indian War, who had charge of the militia at Concord at the time we are considering. It was on his premises that the store and ammunition were concealed which General Gage sent out troops to seize, and thus produced the skirmishes at Lexington and Concord.
2. Paul Revere was one of the most zealous and efficient of the "Sons of Liberty" in New England, a native of Boston, and then forty years of age. He had served as lieutenant of artillery at Fort Edward, on the Upper Hudson, in the French and Indian War. He became a jeweler and an expert copper-plate engraver. One of his most popular pictures was "The Boston Massacre," 1770. The Continental Congress employed Revere to engrave the plates for the Continental paper currency. Early in 1775 the Provincial Congress of Massachusetts sent him to Philadelphia to learn the art of making gunpowder. Joseph Warren, then President of the Massachusetts Provincial Congress, chose Revere as an absolutely trustworthy messenger to carry words of warning to the inhabitants of Lexington and Concord, and to Adams and Hancock, advising them of impending peril. He was now on that errand.
3. The group of objects in the engraving on page 21 comprises the buildings near which the famous skirmish at Lexington occurred; a portrait of Jonathan Harrington, the fifer on the Green on the morning of April 19th, 1775, and the monument erected to the memory of the Americans slain on that occasion.

The largest of the buildings seen in the pictures was the meeting-house, and the other, with two chimneys, was Buckman's Tavern. This view of the locality is drawn from a sketch made by Earle, an artist, on the morning after the fight, in which he represented the skirmish as it occurred in front of these buildings, well toward the left. The monument stands on the spot where most of the patriots were slain.
4. This monument is depicted in the engraving on page 21, from a sketch made by the author in October 1848. The following is a copy of the inscription upon it:

"Sacred to the Liberty and the Rights of Mankind!!! The Freedom and Independence of America—sealed and defended with the blood of her sons. The Monument is erected by the Inhabitants of Lexington, under the Patronage and at the expense of the Commonwealth of Massachusetts, to the memory of their Fellow-citizens, Ensign Robert Monroe, Jonas Parker, Samuel Hadley, Jonathan Harrington, Jr., Isaac Murry, Caleb Harrington, and John Brown, of Lexington, and Asahel Porter, of Woburn, who fell on the Field, the first victims of the sword of British Tyranny and Oppression, on the morning of the ever-memorable Nineteenth of April, An. Dom. 1775. The Die was cast!!! The blood of the Martyrs in the Cause of God and their Country was the cement of the Union of these States, then Colonies, and gave the Spring to the Spirit, Firmness, and Resolution of their Fellow-citizens. They rose as one man to revenge their Brethren's blood, and at the point of the Sword to assert and defend their native Rights. They nobly dared to be Free!!! The Contest was long, bloody, and affecting. Righteous Heaven affirmed the Solemn Appeal. Victory crowned the Americans, and the Peace, Liberty, and Independence of the United States of American was their glorious Reward. Built in the year 1799."

5. "On the evening of April 18th," said Mrs. Chandler, "some British officers, who had been informed where those patriots were, came to Lexington and inquired of a woman whom they met for 'Mr. Clarke's house.' She pointed to the parsonage, but in a moment, suspecting their design, she called to them and inquired if it was Clarke's Tavern they were in quest of. Uninformed whether it was a *tavern* or a *parsonage* where their intended victims were domiciled, the officers replied, 'Yes; Clarke's Tavern.'

'Oh,' said the woman, 'Clarke's Tavern is in that direction,' pointing toward East Lexington.

'As soon as the officers departed the woman hastened to inform the patriots of their danger, when they immediately arose and fled to Woburn, Dorothy Quincy, the intended wife of Hancock, who was with them, accompanying them in their flight. Paul Revere soon afterward arrived and confirmed the suspicions of the patriotic woman.'"

Chapter II

6. Robert Aitkin was a highly esteemed citizen of Philadelphia, and suffered from British oppression because of his patriotic labors in behalf of his country during the war for independence. In 1782, Bibles being scarce and very high in price on account of the war, he printed an edition of the Scriptures. The Continental Congress appointed Reverends Mr. White (afterward Bishop) and Duffield to examine it. They reported favorably, and Congress, by resolution, commended Aitkin's edition of the Bible to the people of the United States. Peace coming soon afterward, Aitkin lost money by the enterprise. His daughter Jane succeeded him in business, and published the Scriptures, translated by Charles Thomson, in four octavo volumes, in 1808.

7. Rev. Jacob Duché, D.D., was a native of Philadelphia, and a clergy-man of the Church of England. At the breaking out of the Revolution he was assistant minister of Christ Church, Philadelphia. He loved freedom, and espoused the patriot cause; and when the First Continental Congress met at Philadelphia, in September, 1774, he was invited to open its proceedings with prayer. He became rector of Christ Church the next year.

Duché was possessed of a timid nature, and when the British took possession of Philadelphia, in the fall of 1777, alarmed by the gloomy outlook, he forsook the Americans, and in a letter to Washington urged him to follow his example. This letter the commander-in-chief transmitted to Congress. Hearing of this, Duché fled to England. His estate was confiscated, and he was banished as a traitor. Thirteen years afterward Duché returned to Philadelphia, when his sins, not being heinous, were forgiven.

8. Extract from the journals of the Continental Congress, Thursday, June 30th, 1782:

"Arms.—Paleways of thirteen pieces, argent and gules [red and white]; a chief azure [blue]; the escutcheon on the breast of the American eagle, displayed proper, holding in his dexter talon an olive branch, and in his sinister a bundle of thirteen arrows, all proper, and in his beak a scroll inscribed with this motto, '*E Pluribus Unum*.'

"For the Crest.—Over the head of the eagle, which appears above the escutcheon, a glory or [golden] breaking through a cloud, proper, and surrounding thirteen stars forming a constellation, argent [white] on an azure [blue] field.

"Reverse.—A pyramid unfinished. In the zenith an eye in a triangle, surrounded with a glory, proper. Over the eye these words, '*Annuit Coeptis*.' On the base of the pyramid the numerical letters MDCCLXXVI. And underneath the following motto: '*Novus ordo Seclorum*,' a 'new order of things.'"

The whole device was intended for a pendent seal, but as a recumbent seal is used, only the obverse side is seen impressed on public documents.

Chapter III

9. The famous high hills of Santee are immense sand-hills, in Sumter District, S.C., extending southward not far below Camden, and are four or five miles in width. They are remarkable for salubrity of climate and for medicinal springs. Here was the residence of General Sumter.

Chapter IV

10. The old Philipse Castle was the first residence or manor-house of the Philipse family. It was built for the double purpose of a dwelling and a defence or castle for the safety of the "Lord of the Manor" and his retainers against hostile Indians.

11. It appears to be a well-authenticated fact of history that young George Washington, when a Virginia colonel, was fascinated by the charms of Mary, a daughter of Colonel Frederick Philipse, a large land-holder on the east bank of the Hudson River, and who at one time was Speaker of the Colonial Assembly of New York. Washington, then twenty-four years of age, while on his way to Boston on official military business, met the young lady at the residence of her sister, Mrs. Beverly Robinson, at New York. Washington's young heart was touched. He lingered; he left her with reluctance, and on his return became the willing guest of Colonel Robinson, where he again lingered as long as duty would allow. He manifested his love for and admiration of Miss Philipse, but it is believed that his natural shyness prevented his offering her his heart and hand at that time. A lover bolder than he pressed his suit and won the maiden. He was Major Roger Morris, a member of Braddock's staff and young Washington's companion-in-arms. They were married, built a fine mansion on Harlem Heights, adhered to the royal cause, and became Tory refugees. In the fall of 1776 Washington occupied their mansion as the headquarters of the Continental army.

12. This mansion, known for more than fifty years past as the "Jumel House," is yet standing, the property of Nelson Chase, Esq., who married an adopted daughter of Madame Jumel, the widow of a Frenchman. Her second husband was the celebrated Aaron Burr. They were married at that mansion by the same minister of the gospel who officiated at the marriage of Burr to his first wife, who was a young widow.

13. This mansion was generally known as the "Upper Van Cortlandt Manor-house," as it was on the Van Cortlandt landed estate. It was built of brick, and when I visited it in 1848 it

stood in the midst of a pleasant lawn, shaded by locust-trees, on the north side of the post-road. There I saw many portraits of the Van Cortlandt family, some of them more than one hundred years old. They were afterward removed to the old manor-house at Croton.

14. In a field a little eastward of the house, when I visited it in 1849, was an oak-tree which had been used as a military whipping-post during the encampment there. It was green and vigorous, and so perfectly symmetrical had its branches grown, that when it was in full foliage it formed a perfect sphere. In a cemetery attached to a little Episcopal church near the manor-house is a white marble monument erected to the memory of John Paulding, one of the captors of Major André.

15. Colonel Samuel Vetch Bayard was a son of Colonel William Bayard, who during the quarrels of the colonies with the mother country, before the war for independence began, was disposed to act with the Whigs. He was associated with John Jay and others as a member of the committee of Fifty of the city of New York; but he finally took sides with the Crown, and his property was confiscated. It was at his former residence, on the bank of the Hudson, in the city of New York, that General Hamilton was brought, wounded, from his duel with Burr on the west side of the river. Colonel Bayard's son, Samuel Vetch, was a fiery young man of twenty-one at this time, and was associated with the De Lanceys in Westchester County in Tory military operations. He died at Wilmot, Nova Scotia, in 1832, at the age of seventy-five years.

16. Colonel Edmund Fanning was a person of considerable note in North Carolina. He married a daughter of Governor William Tryon while the latter was the chief magistrate of that colony. Fanning was Tryon's secretary, came with him to New York, and during the war for independence he was actively engaged in the military service of the Crown. He raised a corps of four hundred and sixty loyalists, which bore the name of the "Associated Refugees," or "King's American Regiment." He was in command of these when the incident related in the text occurred. Colonel Fanning's property in North Carolina was confiscated in 1779. In 1782 he was surveyor-general at New York. In the fall of 1783 he went to Nova Scotia and became councillor and lieutenant governor of that colony. In 1786 he was appointed lieutenant governor of Prince Edward's Island, and held the office nearly twenty years. He died in London in February 1818.

17. There is doubt about the real character of Joshua Hett Smith. He was either a dupe or a willing associate of Benedict Arnold in the plot of Arnold and André. He with two others conveyed Major André from the *Vulture* to the shore near Haverstraw to have a midnight conference with Arnold. The conference between the plotters the next day was held at Smith's house. He furnished André with a suit of clothes for his disguise, and he accompanied André across the Hudson and some distance on his journey toward New York. Smith, suspected of complicity in the plot, was tried by a military court, and was acquitted for want of evidence to convict; but he was taken into custody by the civil authority of the State of New York and committed to prison. There he lay by several months, when he escaped to New York in the disguise of a woman. He went to England at the close of the war. In 1808 Smith published in London what he styled "An Authentick Narrative of the Causes which Led to the Death of Major André." Smith died in New York in 1818.

18. This old church, yet (1888) standing and preserved in its ancient characteristics, is a curiosity. It is built of brick imported from Holland for the purpose. On the little spire still turns the flag-shaped vane of sheet iron in which is cut the monogram of the founder [a capital V and F melded together, his name being spelt in Dutch Vedryck Felypsen], and in

the little belfry yet hangs the bell, bearing the inscription in Latin, "IF GOD BE WITH US, WHO CAN BE AGAINST US?"

On the summit of a gentle slope in the cemetery which surrounds the old church rest the remains of the immediate family of Washington Irving, who made the locality famous. There lie the remains of his parents, brothers, sisters, and nurse. His remains were buried by the side of those of his mother, in fulfillment of his request. All the graves are marked by small upright slabs of white marble. At the old church is the entrance to the famous "Sleepy Hollow."

Chapter V

19. Major James Livingston, distantly related to Chancellor Robert R. Livingston. He was born in Canada, and possessed considerable influence among the Canadians. He was made colonel of a regiment of Canadian refugees, who joined the army under General Montgomery in his invasion of Canada, late in 1775. He led in the capture of Fort Chambly. Colonel Livingston participated in the attack on Quebec, where Montgomery was killed. He served in the army until the close of the war. Although his residence was at Montreal, he died in Saratoga County late in 1832.

20. These were mercenary troops, hired by the British Government of German princes to fight British subjects in America. They were under the chief command of General, the Baron de Riedesel, sent by the Duke of Brunswick.

Chapter VI

21. Not so many. It was occupied by a garrison of one hundred and sixty-five men under the command of Captain McPherson, of Lord Rawdon's British army. A small detachment of dragoons from Charleston had just joined them. McPherson had no artillery, but momentarily expecting assistance from Rawdon, he felt secure.

22. These were from the East Indies. They were presented to Mrs. Motte's brother, Miles Brewton, by an East India sea-captain. After her brother's death, they came into the possession of Mrs. Motte.

Chapter VII

23. This famous tavern was built by Stephen Fay about the year 1768, in the center of the village of Bennington, Vt. During the early period of the settlement of the State this tavern was a great resort for emigrants and travellers, and was widely known as the headquarters of the leaders of the original settlers in the great controversy concerning this region, which was known by the title of "the New Hampshire Grants." Ethan Allen made his home at that house for several years.

On the top of the high sign-post of Landlord Fay's tavern was placed the stuffed skin of a catamount or panther, from which the name of "Catamount Tavern" was derived. The tavern was the seat of justice where offenders against the rights of original settlers on the Grants were tried, and it was sometimes the scene of the infliction of summary justice.

The quarrel was between the civil authorities of the province of New York and the original settlers, the former claiming not only territorial jurisdiction over the domain, but the right to dispossess the settlers. A Dr. Adams, who was one of the early proprietors of land there, suddenly took sides with the New Yorkers. For this offence he was seized and carried to the Catamount Tavern, fifteen miles from his home. There a committee heard his defence, and then ordered him to be tied in an armchair and hoisted up to the sign, twenty-five feet above, whereon stood the stuffed panther, with its grinning mouth toward New York. There the doctor was suspended for two hours, a spectacle that created great merriment among a crowd of spectators. When he was released he was admonished to "go and sin no more."

From the Catamount Tavern went forth the summons from Colonel Ethan Allen, on the morning of May 3rd, 1775, for the mustering of the Green Mountain Boys for the capture of Ticonderoga.

CHAPTER VIII

24. Forty Fort, so called in honor of the first forty emigrants from Connecticut to the Wyoming Valley, was then little more than a weak blockhouse.
25. Wintermoot's Fort was the barricaded home of Wintermoot, a Tory, in the upper part of the Wyoming Valley. When I was in Hamilton, in Canada, in 1860, I saw Mrs. Hannah Aikman, mother of Mr. Michael Aikman, a small, delicate woman, but of clear mind, and then ninety-one years of age. Her family were among the Tory refugees who settled in the Canadian peninsula. They were in Wintermoot's Fort at the time of the invasion. She gave me a graphic account of their flight from the Wyoming Valley, after the battle there, and their sufferings in their forest journey to Niagara. I told her of my visit to the Wyoming Valley, and when I described Wintermoot's home as she remembered it, and spoke of the Bennetts, the Dennisons, the Hallenbacks, the Slocums, and the Dorrances, whom she knew, her eyes brightened, and she said it seemed as if some of her old neighbors had come to see her. Her maiden name was Showers.
26. On May 11th, 1866, Samuel Kennedy, the last survivor of the massacre at Wyoming, died near York Springs, Adams County, Pa. His father was absent at the time of the massacre. His mother and her three children, of whom Samuel was the eldest, after hiding in a wheat-field surrounded by Indians all night, finally escaped. Samuel was then five years of age. He was in his ninety-third year when he died.

CHAPTER IX

27. Huck was sent out with about four hundred mounted Tories, instructed to "push the rebels to the utmost." This he did with alacrity and great cruelty. Loaded with spoils, he returned to the British camp at Rocky Mount, near the right bank of the Catawba River. Again he went out on his destructive errand. On a hot night in July he was encamped in a lane on a plantation. A detachment of about one hundred and thirty men, sent by Sumter, surprised the sleepers. The patriots entered the lane at each end and fell upon Huck's motley troopers. Huck and a Tory militia colonel were killed, and the rest of the forces were dispersed. They were pursued, and within four hours that Tory army was completely dissolved.
28. I visited Rocky Mount soon after this interview. It is an eminence about two miles from the Catawba River, and very near the fine residence, at that time, of Mrs. Barksdale, widow of a South Carolina statesman, who had been accidentally killed not long before my visit.

Hanging Rock is a huge conglomerate bowlder lying upon the verge of the high bank of a small stream, one hundred feet above it.
29. A small stream that falls into the Catawba River a little above the Great Falls.

CHAPTER X

30. Flora Macdonald, daughter of a "gentleman" farmer, was born on Uist, one of the Hebrides or Western Islands, off the coast of Scotland, about 1720. After the battle of Culloden, in 1746, Prince Charles Edward, the Young Pretender to the throne of Scotland, became a fugitive. He was hunted from place to place by the royal troops. The imagination of Flora, then a school-girl, was excited by the stories which daily reached her ears of the heroism and sufferings of the prince, and her loyalty impelled her to attempt to aid him in escaping from his pursuers. She succeeded; was arrested, imprisoned, and pardoned. She married a kinsman in 1750, and in 1774 they emigrated to America. She died in 1790.
31. Sir Walter Scott wrote: "It is remarkable that this distinguished lady signed her name Flory instead of the more classical orthography. Her marriage contract, which is in my possession, bears the name spelled *Flory*."
32. Writing to Mrs. Thrale, Johnson said, alluding to her romantic act: "She must then have been a very young lady; she is not now old; of a pleasing person and elegant behavior. She told me she thought herself honored by my visit, and I am sure that whatever regard she bestowed on me was liberally repaid."

The portrait of Flora Macdonald given in this volume is said to have been painted in London for Commodore Smith, in whose ship she had been brought prisoner from Scotland. She was then about twenty-seven years of age.

CHAPTER XI

33. Will Lee, or "Billy," as he was usually called, was Washington's huntsman before the Revolution; was his favorite body-servant during the war for independence; and was well provided for by his master in his will. He died at a very advanced age about 1828. Washington left him a house to live in and a pension of one hundred and fifty dollars a year. He became a "spoiled child of fortune;" quite intemperate during the later years of his life, and finally died from an attack of *delirium tremens*. On all occasions during the war Washington entrusted to Billy's keeping his most precious papers.

CHAPTER XII

34. The object of this raid on the New England coast was to call back the troops under Washington, then on their campaign against Cornwallis, in Virginia. Arnold laid almost the whole town of New London in ashes. Fifteen vessels, with the effects of the fleeing inhabitants, escaped up the river. The property destroyed was valued at nearly half a million dollars. It is said that Arnold stood in the belfry of a church, almost in sight of his birthplace, at Norwich, and saw the burning of the town with the coolness of a Nero. In 1793 the General Assembly of Connecticut granted five hundred thousand acres of land in the "Western Reserve," Ohio, for the benefit of sufferers from conflagrations on the New

England coast during the old war for independence. This tract was known as "The Fire Lands."–See Lossing's *Cyclopoedia of United States History.*

CHAPTER XIII

35. The headquarters is under the protecting care of the Washington Association of New Jersey, who is composed of patriotic citizens of that State. It is becoming an attractive depository of precious relics of the old war for independence, especially of rare autograph letters and documents. The association gave a grand reception on June 28th, 1888, on the one hundred and tenth anniversary of the battle of Monmouth, near Freehold, N.J. The reception was under the patronage of twelve matrons, the queens of leading families in New Jersey. The headquarters is, happily, secured from neglect and change of features, as it is no longer private property.

36. Judge Ford was mistaken in the personality of the expert cavalry officer. Count Pulaski had been killed at Savannah in October previous to the formation of the encampment at Morristown. His legion was marched to the northward after his death and distributed among various bodies of the Continental Army. It is probable that the officers of that admirably disciplined corps were employed as disciplinarians of mounted men in the army, and that the officer who performed such feats at Morristown was confounded in Judge Ford's mind with Pulaski himself, being of Pulaski's legion, unmindful of the evident anachronism.

37. "Immediately after the arrival of Mrs. Washington at headquarters, some of the principal ladies of Morristown made her a formal visit together, to welcome her to their society. Dressed in their most elegant attire, and wearing their jewels and other ornaments, they were ushered into the presence of the distinguished lady, by whom they were cordially received. They were surprised to find her habited in a very plain gown made of home-made stuff, a white kerchief covering her neck and bosom, a neat cap, and no other ornament than a gold wedding ring. While with her right hand she gave each a kindly greeting, in her left hand she held a half-knit stocking, the ball of yarn lying in an outside pocket hanging by her side. They were still more surprised, when seated, to observe the dignified little woman, while engaged in animate conversation with them, making them feel at ease, plying her knitting-needles incessantly, while they spent the hour in her presence with idle fingers.

"These ladies and others of the village joined Mrs. Washington most heartily in schemes and labors for the alleviation of the sick in camp; and, with the wives of other officers, made an agreeable social circle during that dreadful winter.

"One of the ladies who first called upon Mrs. Washington wrote to a friend: 'Her gracious and cheerful manners delighted us all; but we felt rebuked by the plainness of her apparel and her example of persistent industry, while we were extravagantly dressed idlers. She seems very wise in experience, kind-hearted and winning in all her ways. She talked much of the sufferings of the poor soldiers, especially of the sick ones. Her heart seemed to be full of compassion for them.'" –*Mary and Martha Washington*, by Benson J. Lossing, p. 193.

CHAPTER XIV

38. Beverly Garrison, a survivor of the conflicts at Forts Clinton and Montgomery, told me that he knew "Captain Molly" and her husband. He was with her husband in Fort Clinton

when it was attacked by the British. When the Americans fled as the enemy was scaling the ramparts, Molly's husband, who was then with the artillery, dropped his match and fled. Molly caught it up, touched off the piece, and scampered away, winning the honor of firing the last gun at Fort Clinton.

CHAPTER XV

39. Son and successor of John Bartram, who established the Garden. He was born in Philadelphia in 1739, and became a famous naturalist. He traveled for nearly five years through the Carolinas, Georgia, and Florida, studying the natural productions of that region. In 1783 he was invited to the chair of botany in the University of Pennsylvania, but ill-health prevented his occupying it. Bartram made a complete list of American birds before the appearance of the famous work of Wilson on ornithology. He assisted Wilson in his labors. Bartram died in 1823.
40. Doctor John Jones was an eminent physician and surgeon, and began the practice early, in New York. He was a surgeon in the army under Sir William Johnson, at the battle of Lake George, in 1775, and attended General, then Baron Dieskau, the French commander, who was wounded and a prisoner. The physicians in New York City agreed for their own dignity to wear their hair in a peculiar *bob*. Young Jones refused to comply, and they refused to consult with him. This brought such ridicule upon them that they were compelled to wear their hair like other gentlemen. In 1780 Doctor Jones settled in Philadelphia, and became the physician of both Washington and Franklin. He was a Quaker.
41. On the eve of Washington's departure from Philadelphia, March, 1797, an article appeared in the *Aurora*, written by a Doctor Lieb, in which the Patriot was charged with using the public money for his private use and of being a traitor to his country. "If ever a nation has been debauched by a man," wrote this wretched partisan, "the American nation has been debauched by Washington. If ever a nation was deceived by a man, the American nation has been deceived by Washington. Let his conduct, then, be an example for future ages. Let it serve to be a warning that no man may be an idol. Let the history of the Federal Government instruct mankind that the mask of patriotism may be worn to conceal the foulest designs against the liberties of the people."

CHAPTER XVI

42. I saw Westford at Mount Vernon ten years later (1858). He was the only surviving slave of Judge Bushrod Washington, the inheritor of Mount Vernon. He went there when his master took possession of the estate in 1802. Although he was set free in 1829, by the will of his master, he never left the estate. He was a dark mulatto, and very intelligent and communicative. Westford was then seventy-two years of age. He died two or three years afterward.

CHAPTER XVIII

43. Doctor Eneas Munson, Sr., was born at New Haven in 1734, and died there in 1826. He first studied divinity, then medicine; was a chaplain in the French and Indian War; became a practicing physician in his native town, and was for half a century a leader in his profession. He was President of the Medical Society of Connecticut and professor in the Medical

School of Yale College from its foundation until his death. He was also a member of his State Legislature often during the Revolution.
44. See sketch of *Headquarters at Morristown*.
45. Colonel Alexander Scammell was a very meritorious officer of the Continental Army. He was a graduate of Harvard College; taught school and practised surveying. He assisted in the surveys for a map of New Hampshire. He became a law student in 1755 with John Sullivan, afterward a general in the Continental Army. At the breaking out of the war he entered the military service; was in the battles of Trenton, Princeton, and Long Island; was distinguished in the battles that resulted in the surrender of Burgoyne, and was soon afterward made adjutant-general of the army. He held that position until 1781. He was in command of a regiment at the siege of Yorktown, where he was slain.
46. See Lossing's *Two Spies*, p. 6, for a fac-simile of a part of this letter.

CHAPTER XIX

47. Joseph Bettys, who became a notorious outlaw, was a native of Saratoga Co., N.Y. He joined the Whigs on the breaking out of the Revolution, and was made a prisoner in the naval battle on Lake Champlain in the fall of 1776. While a captive in Canada he was induced to join the royal standard, and was created an ensign. He became a notorious spy, and having been caught by the Americans, he was at one time conducted to the gallows, but in answer to the prayers of his aged parents Washington granted him a reprieve on condition of his thoroughly reforming. But he immediately joined the enemy, and for a long time his cold-blooded murders, his plundering and incendiarism made the name of "Joe Bettys" a terror of the whole region around Albany. He was captured and hung as a spy and traitor at Albany in 1782.

CHAPTER XXI

48. Edmund Charles Genet was born in France in 1763, and died at Greenbush (opposite Albany) in 1834. He was brought up in the French court, and was attached to several embassies in succession at an early period of his life. He had just returned from a mission at St. Petersburg, when, ever holding republican political sentiments, he was appointed by the French Revolutionary Government minister to the United States. His diplomatic career in the United States was so offensive that the President demanded his recall. His country was then scourged by the Reign of Terror, and he dared not return. He remained in the United States, became a naturalized citizen, and married a daughter of Governor George Clinton. He became a most useful and distinguished citizen of our Republic. His second wife was a daughter of Samuel Osgood, the first postmaster-general of the United States.
49. William Cunningham, the British provost-marshal in New York and Philadelphia while those cities were occupied by the British army, was an Irishman possessed of a brutal nature, made more brutal by constant indulgence in the use of intoxicating liquors. There seems to be ample evidence to prove that Cunningham was acting under the immediate direction of official power, higher than that of the military power in America. The most humane General Howe, within whose military jurisdiction Cunningham was employed, tried to restrain his cruelty, but could not. Cunningham's career in New York and Philadelphia furnishes materials for one of the darkest pages in British history.

Other Books
by Benson J. Lossing
Prepared by Michael C. Scoggins

Benson J. Lossing wrote or co-wrote some fifty separate titles during his lifetime, and he also wrote many articles and memorials that were subsequently reprinted as pamphlets or booklets. In addition, Lossing illustrated and annotated a significant number of works by other authors. Lossing's books were very popular in nineteenth-century America, and many of them went through several reprints during his lifetime. In the years since his death, most of his books have been reprinted numerous times by a variety of publishers, often under somewhat different titles and with additional material added from other sources. Unless otherwise noted, all books were written and illustrated by Lossing.

The sheer number of reprints and revised editions of Lossing's books published in the last 165 years makes compiling a comprehensive and exhaustive bibliography difficult; for that reason, this list includes only the original editions of Lossing's works and some of the more important reprints and posthumous editions, along with other books that he illustrated, edited or annotated. Entries are arranged chronologically in order of publication. The information contained in this bibliography was compiled from published Lossing biographies, the Library of Congress online catalog, several university library catalogs, used bookstore listings and other sources.

Outline History of the Fine Arts, embracing a view of the rise, progress, and influence of the arts among different nations, ancient and modern, with notices of the character and works of many celebrated artists; in five parts. [Harpers Family Library No. 105.] (New York: Harper & Brothers, 1840)

Seventeen Hundred and Seventy-Six; or, the War of Independence; a history of the Anglo-Americans, from the period of the union of the colonies against the French, to the inauguration of Washington, the first President of the United States of America. (2 vols. New York: Edward Walker, 1846–1847)

Lives of the Presidents of the United States, embracing a brief history of the principal events of their respective administrations. (New York: H. Phelps, 1847)

Biographical Sketches of the Signers of the Declaration of American Independence: the Declaration historically considered; and a sketch of the leading events connected with the adoption of the Articles of Confederation, and the Federal Constitution. (New York: J.C. Derby, 1848)

A Pictorial Description of Ohio: comprising a sketch of its physical geography, history, political divisions, resources, government and constitution, antiquities, public lands, etc. [Illustrated by maps and forty engravings.] (New York: Ensigns & Thayer, 1849)

The Twelve Stars of our Republic: our nation's gift-book to her young citizens. [With Edwin Williams.] (New York: Edward Walker, 1850)

The Pictorial Field-Book of the American Revolution; or, illustrations, by pen and pencil, of the history, biography, scenery, relics, and traditions of the War for Independence. [Illustrated by Lossing and Barritt.] (2 vols. New York: Harper & Brothers, 1850–1852)

A Pictorial History of the United States, for schools and families. [Illustrated with over two hundred engravings.] (New York: F.J. Huntington, Mason Brothers, 1854)

The National History of the United States, from the period of the union of the colonies against the French, to the inauguration of Washington: together with historical sketches of the continental presidents and an account of the public property of the United States. (2 vols. New York: Edward Walker, 1855)

Our Countrymen; or, brief memoirs of eminent Americans. (New York: American Publishers Corp., 1855)

The Old Farm and the New Farm: a political allegory. [By Francis Hopkinson, with an introduction and historical notes by Benson J. Lossing.] (New York: Dana, 1857)

Eminent Americans: comprising brief biographies of three hundred and thirty distinguished persons. [Illustrated with over one hundred fine portraits, chiefly by Lossing and Barritt.] (New York: Mason Brothers, 1857)

A Primary History of the United States, for schools and families. [Illustrated with numerous engravings.] (New York: Mason Brothers, 1857)

The Statesman's Manual: containing the addresses and messages of the presidents of the United States, inaugural, annual, and special, from 1789 to 1858; with a memoir of each of the presidents, and a history of their administrations; also treaties between the United States and foreign powers, Constitution of the United States, presidents' proclamations, and other important documents and statistical information. [Compiled from official sources by Edwin Williams and Benson J. Lossing; embellished with portraits of the presidents, engraved on steel.] (Rev. and enl. ed., 4 vols. New York: Edward Walker, 1858)

A Pictorial History of the United States, for schools and families. [With over two hundred illustrations.] (New York: Mason Brothers, 1858; San Francisco: H.H. Bancroft & Co., 1858)

Diary of Washington: from the first day of October, 1789, to the tenth day of March, 1790. [Edited by Lossing.] (New York: [Charles B. Richardson & Co.?], 1858)

Memoirs of Washington, by his adopted son, George Wahington Parke Custis, with a memoir of the author, by his daughter, and illustrative and explanatory notes. (Philadelphia: Englewood Publishing Company, 1859)

Mount Vernon and Its Associations, historical, biographical, and pictorial. [Illustrated by numerous engravings, chiefly from original drawings by the author, engraved by Lossing and Barritt.] (New York: W.A. Townsend, 1859)

The Life and Times of Philip Schuyler. (2 vols. New York: Mason Brothers, 1860)

Life of Washington: a biography personal, military and political. [Illustrated by Lossing.] (3 vols. New York: Virtue & Company, 1860)

M'Fingal: an epic poem. [By John Trumbull, with introduction and notes by Lossing.] (New York: G.P. Putnam, 1860)

The Diary of George Washington from 1789–1791; embracing the opening of the first Congress, and his tours through New England, Long Island, and the southern states. Together with his journal of a tour to the Ohio, in 1753. [Edited and annotated by Lossing.] (New York: Charles B. Richardson & Co., 1860)

Cadet Life at West Point, by an officer of the United States Army, with a descriptive sketch of West Point by Benson J. Lossing. [By George Crockett Strong and Benson J. Lossing.] (Boston: T.O.H.P. Burnham, 1862)

The League of States. [Pamphlet reprint of Lossing's article in *Harper's* magazine, January 1863.] (New York: Charles B. Richardson & Co., 1863)

A Common-School History of the United States, from its earliest period to the present time. (New York: Mason Brothers, 1864)

Martha Washington. (New York: J.C. Buttre, 1865)

The Home of Washington and its Associations, historical, biographical, and pictorial. [Revised and enlarged edition of *Mount Vernon*]. (New York: W.A. Townsend, 1865)

The Hudson, from the Wilderness to the Sea. [Illustrated with 306 engravings on wood, from drawings by the author, and a frontispiece on steel.] (New York: Virtue and Yorston, 1866; Troy, NY: H.B. Nims & Co., 1866)

The Pictorial Field Book of the Civil War in the United States of America: journeys through the battlefields in the wake of conflict. [Illustrated by many hundred engravings on wood by Lossing and Barritt, from sketches by the author and others.] (3 vols. Vol. 1, Philadelphia: George W. Childs, 1866; Vols. 2 and 3, Hartford, 1869)

Vassar College and Its Founder. [Illustrated by John F. Runge.] (New York: C.A. Alvord, 1867)

Pictorial Field Book of the War of 1812; or illustrations by pen and pencil, of the history, biography, scenery, relics and traditions of the last War for American Independence. [Illustrated by Lossing.] (New York: Harper & Brothers, 1868)

The Life, Campaigns and Battles of General Ulysses S. Grant, comprising a full and authentic account of the famous soldier, from his earliest boyhood to the present time. [By Julian K. Lark, illustrated by Lossing.] (New York: L. Bill, 1868; Chicago: C. Bill, 1868)

Poems. [By William Wilson; edited by Lossing, with biography.] (Poughkeepsie, NY: Archibald Wilson, 1869)

Memoir of Lieut.-Col. John T. Greble, of the United States Army. (Philadelphia: privately printed, 1870)

Washington and the American Republic. (New York: Virtue & Yorston, 1870)

A History of England, political, military and social, from the earliest times to the present. (New York: G.P. Putnam, 1871)

A Memorial of Alexander Anderson, M.D., the first engraver on wood in America; read before the New York Historical Society, Oct. 5, 1870. (New York: printed for the New York Historical Society, 1872)

The American Historical Record, and repertory of notes and queries, concerning the history and antiquities of America and biography of Americans. [Edited by Lossing.] (3 vols. Philadelphia: Chase & Town, 1872–1874)

Our Country: a household history for all readers, from the discovery of America to the present time. [With five hundred illustrations by Felix O.C. Darley.] (3 vols. New York: Johnson & Miles, 1873)

History of the United States of America. [By J.A. Spencer, D.D.; continued to July 4, 1876, by Benson J. Lossing.] (Centennial edition, 4 vols. New York: Johnson, Wilson, 1874–1876)

Hull's Surrender of Detroit. [Reprinted, with additions, from *Potter's American Monthly*, August 1875.] (Philadelphia: J.E. Potter and Company, 1875)

The American Centenary: a history of the progress of the republic of the United States during the first one hundred years of its existence. (Philadelphia: Porter & Coates, 1876)

Centenniel Edition of the History of the United States, from the discovery of the American continent to the present time, with scenes and events in the life and times of Washington to which is added the portraits and autographs of the presidents of a century. [With over four hundred illustrations.] (Hartford, CT: Thomas Belknap, 1876)

History of American Industries and Arts. [Illustrated with numerous engravings on steel.] (Philadelphia: Porter & Coates, 1878)

The Story of the United States Navy, for boys. [Illustrated.] (New York: Harper & Brothers, 1880)

Harper's Popular Cyclopedia of United States History, from the aboriginal period to 1876, containing brief sketches of important events and conspicuous actors. [With over one thousand illustrations by Felix O.C. Darley and others] (2 vols. New York: Harper & Brothers, 1881)

The Biography of James A. Garfield, late president of the United States. [Illustrated.] (New York: H.S. Goodspeed & Co., 1882)

History of New York City: embracing an outline of events from 1609 to 1830, and a full account of its development from 1830 to 1884. [Illustrated with portraits, views of parks, buildings, etc., engraved on steel by Perine.] (2 vols. New York: G.E. Perine, 1884)

A Family History of the United States, from the discovery of the American continent to the present time. (New York: Gay Brothers & Company, 1884)

Mary and Martha, the mother and wife of George Washington. [Illustrated with facsimiles of pen-and-ink drawings by H. Rosa.] (New York: Harper & Brothers, 1886)

Two Spies: Nathan Hale and John André. (New York: D. Appleton & Co., 1886)

In Memory of John B. Moreau: proceedings of the New York Historical Society upon the death of the late Mr. John B. Moreau. (New York: printed for the New York Historical Society, 1886)

The Empire State, a compendious history of the commonwealth of New York. [Illustrated with facsimiles of 335 pen-and-ink drawings by H. Rosa.] (New York: Funk & Wagnalls, 1887)

Hours with the Living Men and Women of the Revolution: a pilgrimage. [Illustrated with facsimiles of pen-and-ink drawings by H. Rosa.] (New York: Funk & Wagnalls, 1889)

Our Great Continent; sketches, picturesque and historic: within and beyond the States. [By Benson J. Lossing, Geo. J. Hagar and other well-known writers.] (2 vols. New York: Gay Brothers & Company, 1889)

The Achievements of Four Centuries, or, the wonderful story of our great continent within and beyond the States: the marvellous and unparalleled progress of the hemisphere of republics, from the landing of Columbus to the present time: historical, statistical and descriptive...the whole forming a grand cycloramic view of the Western world. [By Benson J. Lossing and other well-known writers.] (New York: Gay Brothers & Company, 1890)

The Countries of the Western World: the governments and people of North, South and Central America, from the landing of Columbus to the present time; pen and pencil pictures of the great wonderlands of our republic, their natural scenery... (New York: Gay Brothers & Company, 1890)

The Marriage of Pocohontas. (New York: John McRae, 1890)

POSTHUMOUS REPRINTS AND REVISED EDITIONS OF LOSSING'S WORKS

Lossing's Story of a Great Nation; or, our country's achievements, military, naval, political, and civil. (New York: Gay Brothers & Company, 1893)

Our Country: a household history of the United States for all readers, from the discovery of America to the present time. [By Benson J. Lossing, LLD; continued from July 4, 1876, by Hugh Craig; with over five hundred illustrations by Felix O.C. Darley.] (3 vols. New York: Johnson & Bailey, 1894)

Harper's Encyclopaedia of United States History from 458 A.D. to 1902, based upon the plan of Benson John Lossing...with special contributions covering every phase of American history and development by eminent authorities...with a preface on the study of American history by Woodrow Wilson. [By Lossing and others.] (10 vols. New York: Harper & Brothers, 1902; revised and reprinted in 1905 and 1912)

A History of the Civil War 1861–65, and the causes that led up to the great conflict. [With photographs by Matthew Brady.] (16 vols. New York: Crown Publishers for War Memorial Association, 1912)

Matthew Brady's Illustrated History of the Civil War 1861–65, and the causes that led up to the great conflict. [Lossing's text, with Brady's photographs replacing Lossing's engravings.] (New York: Fairfax Press, 1972, 1977)

The Field Book of the American Revolution. 2 vols. (Cottonport, LA: Polyanthos, 1972)

Matthew Brady's Illustrated History of the Civil War, with 737 Brady photographs. [Lossing's text and Brady's photographs.] (New York: Random House Value Publishing, 1988)

An Early view of the Shakers: Benson John Lossing and the Harper's article of July 1857, with reproductions of the original sketches and watercolors. [Edited by Don Gifford; foreword by June Sprigg.] (Hanover: published for Hancock Shaker Village by University Press of New England, 1989)

Matthew Brady's Illustrated History of the Civil War, with his war photographs and paintings by military artists. (New York: Gramercy Press, 1994; Portland Press, paperback 1995, hardback 1996)